Advanced Praise for *Fraud and Fiction*

"I loved *Fire and Fury*, but even the author admitted that he only wrote what the president's advisors told him. Eddie Scarry, one of Washington's best political writers, shows where they were wrong."

—Ann Coulter, *New York Times* Bestselling Author

"Eddie Scarry has gotten exactly to the heart of the problem with the liberal media in the Trump era. They have become obsessed with trying to overthrow an elected President of the United States. They hate him—but in the ultimate irony they need him for ratings. So what once were hard news outlets in television, print, and online have become anti-Trump propaganda machines. Eddie has plunged into this thicket of media craziness and written an astute analysis of what he finds. This is a book that is as witty as it is spot-on. A must-read in the Trump era."

—Jeffrey Lord, Reagan White House
Associate Political Director and Contributing
Editor of *The American Spectator*

THE REAL TRUTH BEHIND *FIRE AND FURY:*
INSIDE THE TRUMP WHITE HOUSE

FRAUD
AND FICTION

EDDIE SCARRY

Post Hill
PRESS

A BOMBARDIER BOOKS BOOK
An Imprint of Post Hill Press
ISBN: 978-1-64293-020-7
ISBN (eBook): 978-1-64293-021-4

Fraud and Fiction
The Real Truth Behind Fire and Fury: Inside the Trump White House
© 2018 by Eddie Scarry
All Rights Reserved

Cover Design by Cody Corcoran

Post Hill Press
New York • Nashville
posthillpress.com

Published in the United States of America

DEDICATION

Dedicated to the national media's burning and undying hatred for President Trump, without which this book would not have been possible.

CONTENTS

INTRODUCTION

Watching a previously obscure author's anti-Trump book blaze around the world, selling millions of copies, based largely on a bunch of lies will go down in history as one of the weirdest things that ever happened in presidential politics. And not just because Michael Wolff's *Fire and Fury* disintegrated when it finally got the scrutiny it deserved, but because it was ever taken seriously at all.

It happened over the course of just barely even two months, which should be a record in the category of bestselling books collapsing to nothing.

We know how it happened.

Wolff's book, had it been written about anyone else, would have been ignored simply because of the unrestrained and fantastical claims it contains: that the president is mentally incapacitated, that he doesn't recognize people he's known for years, that the rest of the executive branch is ready to invoke the 25th Amendment.

This is the type of melodrama that Shonda Rhimes lays on infinitely thick in any one of her TV shows. But a little-known media journalist crammed it into a book and suddenly the nation was breaking out in hives.

To name a few of the lies in *Fire and Fury*:

- President Trump is not, as Wolff's book alluded, in mental decline. It's in fact, the opposite, as demonstrated by Trump's White House physician, Dr. Ronny Jackson, who was first appointed to his role by former president Barack Obama. After Wolff's book came out, Jackson told a room of reporters that not only did he not have any doubts about Trump's mental acuity, but he administered a cognitive test at the request of Trump and the president received a perfect score.

- Trump didn't spend nearly two years running a race for president that he hoped to lose. The idea is preposterous and, contrary to what Wolff says, it would have irreparably wrecked the luxury and success brand Trump spent his whole adult life creating. When you campaign on working-class platform (i.e., an appeal to the people who cannot afford to go to Trump's properties) and lose, how does that translate into 100,000-dollar-plus golf club memberships? It doesn't.

- There is no evidence Nikki Haley is or was ever having an affair with Trump, a claim about which Wolff titillated the media during his book tour. After pushing the rumor for days, even he finally admitted that he did not know if Trump was having an affair, despite saying previously that he was certain of it. But this is like yelling that there's a bomb on a crowded subway, watching passengers get trampled to death in a panicked stampede, and then confessing that it was just a joke. There is no point in trying to take back irreparable damage.

- White House policy adviser Stephen Miller is not, per *Fire and Fury*, an illiterate caveman. If anything—and any reporter worth a damn will tell you this—Miller is possibly the White House's most studied adviser and has demonstrated his mastery of immigration policy by cleaning the press briefing room floor with CNN correspondent Jim Acosta's head.

- Wolff didn't go into his book project "having accepted no rules nor having made any promises," as he states at the beginning of his book. He explicitly told the White House he planned to write a book that would show Trump in a way that the public hadn't seen before. Instead, Wolff wrote everything the media have been saying since 2015: that Trump is psychologically manic, hopelessly ignorant, and, oh, by the way, his election victory was a lark. Wolf ingratiated himself to the White House and then double-crossed them with a fake book.

Shortly before this book went to print, President Trump called me to say what he had said before: Michael Wolff had no access to him for *Fire and Fury*.

"That book was a total fraud," Trump told me on the phone. "It was a disgrace. It was really disgraceful."

He said that a lot of people in his orbit were "maligned" by Wolff and that he never met with the author.

Wolff has said he spent about three hours total with Trump over the course of the time he was writing his book, and that he has audio recordings of interviews he conducted but he has never made those public.

"He never met me," said Trump. "He called; I said, I don't want to meet with him. I said I didn't think it was appropriate. He was never in the Oval Office."

He acknowledged that ousted White House adviser Steve Bannon, however, did frequently go to Wolff to give interviews. But he said nobody knew that was happening until after *Fire and Fury* published.

Trump changed the subject several times to vent about the national media's coverage of his administration, particularly after it was announced that he had agreed to meet with North Korean dictator Kim Jong-un.

"I get it done," Trump said, adding that his predecessor, President Obama, couldn't have done it. "Obama didn't even know [Kim] was alive."

He specifically singled out CNN's coverage, which he said was negative because its chief executive Jeff Zucker is "a total joke" and "a real loser."

But we ended our eight-minute phone call with some final thoughts on Wolff and his book.

"It was a total con job," Trump said.

"I may bring a lawsuit," he said. And referring to this book and how it relates to *Fire and Fury*, he said, "I hope it decimates the crap out of it."

* * *

None of this could have happened without the press, so much of it consumed with hatred for Trump, willing to buy what Wolff was selling.

As outlandish and unbelievable as Wolff's book was, no real convincing was needed for the national media to legitimize it. The book confirmed what they wanted to be true ever since Trump launched his campaign for president in June 2015.

News outlets called Wolff's book "explosive" (CBS News), made lists of its biggest "revelations" (*Newsweek*), and hyped its "juicy tale" (*The Washington Post*).

Less than two weeks after the book published, a production company purchased the rights to turn it into a television show.

The story was too good to check. At least not before its most sensational elements had been foisted onto the public.

The absurdity of Wolff's book was captured in perfect form when a humorist on Twitter shared an image of what he said was a page from *Fire and Fury* describing Trump wanting to watch a 24-hour live feed of gorillas on his television in the White House.

"Wow, this extract from Wolff's book is a shocking insight into Trump's mind," tweeted Ben Ward, a cartoonist who goes by "pixelatedboat." The mock-page said that Trump "complained" during his first night in the White House "that the TV in his bedroom was broken because it didn't have 'the gorilla channel.'" It went on to say that "White House staff" strung together a bunch of gorilla documentaries to play on the TV in order to satisfy the president.

Ward's tweet has since been shared by others more than 26,000 times.

At the time, MSNBC contributor and liberal activist Scott Dworkin stupidly promoted the joke as if it were real. "Trump was mad cuz his tv wasn't getting 'the gorilla channel,'" Dworkin tweeted. "Doesn't exist."

Thanks to Dworkin and others who viewed the fake page in earnest, several news and fact-checking websites, including the myth-debunking site Snopes, had to demonstrate that it wasn't real.

Fire and Fury did, eventually, get the skepticism it deserved, but not until its most scandalous claims had been aired, wreaking havoc on the White House and the country for nearly a month.

Thanks to the media stoking Wolff's shocking book, no matter how ridiculous its contents, everyone was left to wonder: *If the president isn't okay, how is our country safe?*

That's a serious question that should terrify even Trump's most unyielding critics.

Having covered the media during the 2016 election, I know the sour political environment that Wolff took advantage of to ensure a book like *Fire and Fury* would strike a chord with journalists, who would then push its message onto the front pages of national newspapers and TV news shows.

Everyone, including Trump's supporters, was stunned by the election. But no one more than the journalists and pundits who make up the national media.

So many of them believed the election's outcome was an actual professional and moral failure and even today, they continue debating what they "missed."

But in the absence of accepting reality, there was Wolff's book to keep open the possibility that Trump's victory was an aberration in history and not the true will of the people.

Though Wolff's book eventually burned out, it damaged Trump's presidency and still nobody knows how it may affect the 2020 election.

This is the truth about the fraud and fiction behind *Fire and Fury*.

CHAPTER 1

MICHAEL WOLFF, EXPLAINED

In the summer of 2015, a copy of *Television Is the New Television: The Unexpected Triumph of Old Media in the Digital Age* was delivered to my desk at *The Washington Examiner*'s office in Washington, D.C.

I saw the book was authored by Michael Wolff, a media columnist whose work I was familiar with but whom I didn't find particularly remarkable. I knew he had a strange preoccupation with the personal and romantic life of Rupert Murdoch, the geriatric CEO of News Corp. And I knew Wolff to be periodically mocked in the now-defunct gossip website *Gawker*.

He used to edit *AdWeek*, before he was fired (and which nobody outside of the advertising and media industry reads).

He founded the news aggregation website *Newser* (which nobody reads).

And he wrote a biography about Murdoch, for those interested in who Murdoch's wives were. (I'm not sure who that is, and it should be nobody.)

After flipping through a few pages of the book, I concluded I couldn't write anything about it for the *Examiner* because a) it wasn't about politics, and b) the book was as exciting as any book about the TV industry could possib-zzzzzz…

Fast-forward two and a half years and Wolff is the number 1 bestselling author, having written the most provocative book about President Trump to date, consuming a month's worth of attention from the national media.[1] It's a true story of drags to riches, a writer undistinguished outside of Manhattan sews together a salacious political book that became a sensation overnight.

It's also a true story about a national media eagerly waiting for someone like Wolff to fulfill all the things they want to believe about Trump: that he is mentally unbalanced, dangerously unfit for office, and that his election is a glitch in history.

Columnists, cable news anchors, and other journalists glommed onto Wolff's *Fire and Fury: Inside the Trump White House* with sticky hands, ready to hold it up as proof that their anti-Trump fever was justified.

To the national media, it still does not matter that Trump, a political novice, won the election in an electoral landslide, having fully captured the mood of the nation at large (rather than just the densely populated coastlines that delivered Hillary Clinton the popular vote).

They said he was a faker, tacky, vulgar, offensive, unserious, unsmart, racist, xenophobic, sexist, and bigoted.

He didn't lose. But for the media, the election was still up for debate, and here was Wolff's book to make their case.

After the book's debut, *New York Times* anti-Trump columnist (excuse the redundancy) Bret Stephens lightly rapped Wolff for the "casual errors of fact" and the "unsourced or unverifiable" stories within the book. That said, he agreed with *Fire and Fury*'s main themes.[2]

"Guess what?" Stephens wrote. "Donald Trump is a raving idiot. Every sentient person knows this, and if Michael Wolff is to be believed, so does most everyone in the White House. So why are we talking about Wolff's book *Fire and Fury* as if it's the news sensation of the decade?"

He went on to make the very original point that Trump is "ignorant, incurious, vain, gauche, bigoted, intemperate, bullying, suggestible, reckless, and morally unfit for his office."

It should be noted that Stephens, who previously held a reputation as a conservative thinker, only has a job at the *Times* because he hates Trump, a requirement for the paper's opinion pages.

In December 2015, by which point Trump was tearing through his Republican primary opponents, and when Stephens was a writer at *The Wall Street Journal*, Stephens insisted that Hillary Clinton was certain to win the general election.

From the column, which took the form of a condescending letter to Republican voters drifting toward Trump: "Let us now pledge to elect Hillary Clinton as the 45th president of the United States.... Let's do this because it's what we want. Maybe secretly, maybe unconsciously, but desperately. We want four—and probably eight—more years of cable-news neuralgia. We want to drive ourselves to work as [radio hosts] Mark Levin or Laura Ingraham scratch our ideological itches until they bleed a little. We want the refiner's fire that is our righteous indignation at a country we claim no longer to recognize—ruled by impostors and overrun by foreigners."[3]

In October, just a few days before the election, Stephens then declared he was leaving the GOP, writing, "I don't see the point of belonging to a party on the increasingly dubious assumption that it's slightly less bad than the opposition. If I can't get my Grand Old Party back, I'd rather help build a new one."[4]

Stephens then checked his mailbox and—*Wow!* A job offer from *The New York Times*!

Stephens was apparently brought on as a conservative who hates Trump to balance out the *Times'* other recent hire, Michelle Goldberg, a liberal who hates Trump.

A few days before Stephens' op-ed on *Fire and Fury*, Goldberg gave her take, which, like Stephens', made the case that Wolff's book told us what she already knew. "[T]he book confirms what is already widely understood," she wrote, "not just that Trump is entirely unfit for the presidency, but that everyone around him knows it."[5]

Goldberg's denunciation of Trump as unfit for office was just the latest example of her bravery. Two months prior, she called for the resignation of Democratic Minnesota Senator Al Franken after a Los Angeles-based radio personality accused him of sexually assaulting her, complete with a several-years-old photograph of him putting his flippers on her breasts while she slept.

"I would mourn Franken's departure from the Senate, but I think he should go, and the [Minnesota] governor should appoint a woman to fill his seat," wrote Goldberg (and please ignore the dumb virtue-signaling about appointing a woman to fill his seat). "The message to men in power about sexual degradation has to be clear: We will replace you."[6]

Stunning as it was that a liberal writer in the nation's most important newspaper would call for a Democrat to resign, the excitement was short lived. After sleeping on it, Goldberg wrote four days later that she was having "second thoughts" about her call to action. "I spent all weekend feeling guilty that I'd called for the sacrifice of an otherwise decent man to make a political point....I am still not sure I made the right call."[7]

lol.

MSNBC's *Morning Joe* co-hosts Mika Brzezinski and Joe Scarborough, along with their cast of regular misfit guests, have spent more than a year wondering about Trump's mental health (except in the case of Donnie Deutsch, who was known to be preoccupied with questions about Trump's penis).[8]

In December 2017, Trump concluded a statement at the White House recognizing Jerusalem as the capital of Israel with the usual, "God bless the United States." There was an obvious slur in his words that *Morning Joe* amplified as evidence of dementia on the next day's show.

"This is not the person that we knew even three years ago.... There's a remarkable change," said Scarborough.[9]

"He seemed like he was almost hanging on to the prompter and hanging on to the words," Brzezinski chimed in. "Something, I don't know...There was a struggle happening."

The Daily Beast columnist and petrified fossil Mike Barnicle, who was on the program, helpfully added, "When you consider his age, his physical condition, he does not look in great physical shape and hasn't for some time." Mind you this is coming from Barnicle, who looks like hardened tree sap rolled in flour.

It turned out that the slurring was likely the cause of dry mouth precipitated by a decongestant that Trump had taken at the recommendation of his doctor. But the *Morning Joe* conversation served as a nice precursor to Wolff's book, which the MSNBC program took as even further license to speculate that Trump's brain was deteriorating.[10]

"[A]fter the shock of Wolff's account of Trump's willful ignorance and intellectual incoherence fades, Americans will be left with the inescapable conclusion that the president is not capable of ful-filling his duties as commander in chief," Scarborough wrote in *The Washington Post* in January. Later in the column, he added, "Mika Brzezinski and I had a tense meeting with Trump following what I considered to be a bumbling debate performance in September 2015. I asked the candidate a blunt question. 'Can you read?'…I am apparently not the only one who has questioned the president's ability to focus on the written word."[11]

On the January 9 edition of MSNBC's *Hardball*, Wolff fed into the anti-Trump media hysteria, telling host Chris Matthews that having Trump in the White House was "a little bit of a tragedy here for the American people."

It's obvious why Wolff was able to go from virtual nobody to number 1 author in an instant. The media had been pushing their horrific suspicions and theories about Trump for more than a year and now here was an "insider" account to prove all of it true. Even if that wasn't Wolff's aim, it was the national media's goal, and the book helped them chase it.

CHAPTER 2

CONFUSED ON HOW WOLFF GOT THE STORY? GOOD!

It would be interesting to see a national survey of what *Fire and Fury* readers' initial thoughts were in the book's opening pages. Michael Wolff's author's note, wherein he explains his supposed methods for writing the book, is so convoluted, so impossible to understand that the note should have included two aspirin at the end.

But confusion was likely the intent.

What Wolff puts forth as a measure of his own transparency is actually an attempt to obfuscate.

By Wolff's telling, he told Trump after the election that he was interested in writing a book on his presidency and that, after given the clear, he took up a "semipermanent seat on a couch in the West Wing." Wolff said he was given this stunning amount of access "having accepted no rules nor having made any promises about what I might or might not write."

But in an interview to promote the book on NBC's *Today*, Wolff admitted he had scammed his subjects. "I certainly said what was ever necessary to get the story," he said.[12]

In response, America's collective conscience said: *Wow, what an asshole!*

CNN anchor Michael Smerconish further demonstrated that the part about Wolff having "accepted no rules nor having made any promises" was either partially or fully untrue. Shortly after the book published, Smerconish confronted Wolff with an email the author had written to a Trump aide wherein he had presented himself as a Trump groupie hoping to carry the president's child.

"Did you tell them that your objective was to humanize the president, that nobody was doing that? That you personally like the president? That you'd be able to change perceptions about the president? That you hope to interview him in a relaxed state?" Smerconish said to Wolff in a January 13 interview.

Wolff confirmed that he had likely said those things in the email.

Smerconish then read from the message Wolff had sent to an unnamed person close to Trump: "What I'm really after is not so much a policy or position interview with the president but an opportunity to humanize him," Wolff said to the Trump aide, according to Smerconish. "Honestly, I don't think there is anybody out there who is doing this or it seems who cares about doing this but I think you know that I like him and I believe I can show him in a way that might actually change perceptions of him...I'm open to anything but the more relaxed the better."

That doesn't sound like someone who "accepted no rules" and made no "promises" about what he "might or might not write." In fact, it sounds like the exact opposite. It sounds like Wolff swindled the White House.

Without accepting that he had not been up front with the White House about his intent in writing the book, Wolff defended himself by accusing Smerconish of "doing the work of the White House to discredit this book."

So, Wolff had apparently made promises to Trump about what his intentions were. Or, at the very least, he made it seem like he was there to tell a harmless story.

We know that's not what he ended up doing.

The author's note in Wolff's book is even worse in explaining how he put his story together:

> *"Many of the accounts of what has happened in the Trump White House are in conflict with one another; many, in Trumpian fashion, are baldly untrue,"* he wrote.

So how are readers supposed to know which accounts are the true ones and which aren't? If Wolff knows there are "baldly untrue" ones, why didn't he ferret those out?

Lack of clarity is useful when you're deceiving people, and that's what Wolff seemed to be striving for. "Those conflicts and that looseness with the truth, if not with reality itself, are an elemental thread of the book," the note continues, sending readers a message that's impossible to interpret as anything other than: *You're on your own in figuring out what any of this means.*

Other lines from Wolff's incomprehensible mess of an explanation:

> *"Sometimes I have let the players offer their versions, in turn allowing the reader to judge them."*

Here Wolff is suggesting he's giving free rein for his sources to speak and that he won't vouch for their veracity.

> *"In other instances, I have, through a consistency in accounts and through sources I have come to trust, settled on a version of events I believe to be true."*

How is the reader supposed to determine the difference between an unfiltered version of events put forth by one of Wolff's sources and the other occasions where he has "settled on a version of events" that he simply decided must be true?

> *"I have also relied on off-the-record interviews, allowing a source to provide a direct quote with the understanding that it was not for attribution."*

As with the rest of the author's note, this part is unclear but what it might mean is that Wolff trusted sources to relay private conversations to him, which, by definition, means that they were not "direct" quotes.

> *"At the same time it is worth noting some of the journalistic conundrums that I faced when dealing with the Trump administration.... These challenges have included dealing with off-the-record or deep-background material that was later casually put on the record."*

Another peculiar phrasing by Wolff, which was, again, probably intended to disguise his writing. What does it mean to "later casually" put something on the record? If Wolff's sources allowed something to be on record after the fact, that's not a conundrum; it makes a journalist's job easier. He seems to be suggesting instead that a source told him something privately, but then went and said it publicly in some capacity, either to the media or to more people in conversation. No one can know.

With this type of unintelligible sourcing, coupled with the outlandish claims in Wolff's book, it should come as no shock that the *Fire and Fury* acknowledgements reserves a special kiss for Wolff's libel lawyer. "A libel reading can be like a visit to the dentist," he wrote. "But in my long experience, no libel lawyer is more nuanced, sensitive and strategic than Eric Rayman. Once again, almost a pleasure."

Rayman was undoubtedly paid well for what must have been a massive undertaking in lawsuit-proofing Wolff's work.

A lengthy review of the book by journalist Jonathan Martin in *The New York Times* tackled Wolff's mindfuck sourcing in the book, calling it "slippery" and rightfully says Wolff "throws his hands up" when it comes to explaining crucial pieces of the book that deserve an answer for how the author was able to get them.[13]

If the sourcing in the book doesn't make sense to a professional journalist, what is the average reader supposed to think?

Nothing. Wolff simply confused them using a bunch of terms that mean nothing to anybody.

Just as he "certainly said what was ever necessary to get the story," he said what was necessary to sell it.

CHAPTER 3

IS IT TRUE? SURE, WHY NOT?!

Large swaths of Michael Wolff's book are so impossibly far-fetched that even a fraction of critical thinking would lead an average person to smartly conclude: *This guy is so full of shit.*

As a quick example, Wolff claims in his book that Hope Hicks, the president's longtime communications aide, and former campaign manager Corey Lewandowksi engaged in an affair, citing a petition to a lawsuit Trump filed against his former political aide Sam Nunberg.[14]

Despite Hicks largely eluding the public eye, there are plenty of photos of the former Ralph Lauren model available online, particularly after she was thrust into the national dialogue by a minor scandal in February centering on an alleged White House aide love interest who had assaulted two of his ex-wives.

Lewandowski has spent far more time in front of the camera than Hicks, and even Stevie Wonder would walk away from his photos knowing he's likely not on the same playing field as a former model.

Hicks, now twenty-nine, is the kind of woman you see in a movie. She's attractive, impeccably dressed, and if you met her, you would want to meet her again just to see her. Even I want to meet her again, and I'm gay.

If Hicks is a natural beauty, Lewandowski, forty-four, is decidedly not.

During the campaign in 2016, Trump sued Nunberg, whom Trump had fired after racist comments resurfaced on his Facebook, claiming that the former aide had breached a confidentiality agreement.[15]

Trump was seeking ten million dollars.

The breach allegedly occurred in May 2016 when Lewandowski informed at least one journalist that Lewandowski and Hicks were seen in a heated back-and-forth on a public street in New York. *The New York Post*'s "Page Six" gossip column broke the story, though it made no mention of an affair.[16]

Nunberg's response to Trump's suit said that Lewandowski and Hicks were parties to a "sordid and apparently illicit affair." The petition reads like an embittered former employee, enumerating all the reasons he no longer supported Trump—after having been fired. His assertion that Lewandowski and Hicks had an affair was so plainly an attempt to inflict more harm on the campaign that had fired him and yet Wolff cited it in his book as a fact.

The very first chapter of Wolff's book is recognized as complete fiction by any honest person working in national politics or media.

(That is, admittedly, a small number.) Wolff's book begins with the curious proposition that Trump, and, in fact, nearly everyone working on his campaign, never intended to win the race.

"Almost everybody in the campaign, still an extremely small outfit, thought of themselves as a clear-eyed team, as realistic about their prospects as perhaps any in politics," Wolff wrote. "The unspoken agreement among them: Not only would Donald Trump not be president, he should probably not be. Conveniently, the former convention meant nobody had to deal with the latter issue."

Assuming this were true, it completely undermines investigations, led by the Justice Department, the news media, and both houses of Congress, into whether the Trump campaign colluded with Russia. If Trump never wanted to win the election, why would his campaign ever have colluded with Russia to sway the race?

The collusion theory is less and less valid, but Wolff's claim about Trump not wanting to win the election is very obviously untrue.

Trump has spent decades talking about issues he believed were ruining America and stunting its potential. Mostly it was unfair trade deals and ineffective leadership. He has never changed his rhetoric in these areas. (Though in what was in every way a stroke of political genius, he intuited ahead of his campaign that preventing the dumping of thousands of illegal immigrants into the country was a winning issue, despite never having really talked about the subject much before.)

Over his lifetime, Trump kept a foot in politics and in 2011, he began serious steps at laying down the foundations for a full re-creation of himself as a possible presidential candidate.

He gave his first political speech in 2011 at the massive Conservative Political Action Conference. He used social media to push his views in the national discourse. And he secured a weekly spot on the morning Fox News show *Fox & Friends* to maintain a constant presence in the minds of the Republican voters across the country, the people he would need to vitalize for a campaign.

These are not things you do if you're unserious about leveraging your celebrity into a legitimate political force.

In the final 100 days of the campaign, Trump spent 50 percent more time in the crucial battleground states than Hillary Clinton, according to NBC News. He made a total of 133 visits to Florida, Pennsylvania, Ohio, North Carolina, Michigan, and Wisconsin. Clinton famously neglected to visit left-leaning Wisconsin even once.

In the last two days of the campaign, Trump stormed through the states he needed, hosting 10 of his mega rallies exactly where they were needed. Election Day of 2016 was held on November 7. The final rally took place in Grand Rapids, Michigan, after midnight. "We're hours away from a once-in-a-lifetime change," Trump said. "Today is our Independence Day, the day the American working class is going to strike back, finally."

If you want to win against all odds, with the Democratic Party, the entire national media and even the Republican Party operating to ensure you fail, you campaign like Trump.

If you don't want to win, you campaign like Mitt Romney in 2012.

Trump ran a campaign like we will never see again in our lifetimes. Despite what the media said about it—that it was "dark," "negative," and "pessimistic"—the voters who decided the campaign's outcome saw it as refreshing, forthcoming, and a desperate correction to the political infrastructure that brought havoc on normal people for decades.

But, according to Wolff, Trump was certain and ready to lose and that even so, "He would come out of this campaign...with a far more powerful brand and untold opportunities."

This is not true. Trump's brand is a luxury label and the people his campaign appealed to were not luxury people. It's not as though he had tapped into a whole new market of working class people who were now eager to set off to the nearest Trump property. Trump's core supporters can't afford to visit those places.

An annual club membership at Mar-a-Lago in Palm Beach, Florida, for example, was 100,000 dollars before Trump won the election, according to *Town & Country* magazine.[17]

I've been to the Trump International hotel in Washington, DC, and know that just three drinks at the bar will quickly set you back 100 bucks. If Trump had lost the race, his high-end brand would have been permanently blackened. When your brand is synonymous with success and winning, how does losing the ultimate campaign factor in?

Wolff claims in *Fire and Fury* that Trump supporter and tech entrepreneur Peter Thiel was ready and willing to partner with former Fox News CEO Roger Ailes on a startup TV venture centered on "Trumpism." The partnership never happened of course, because Ailes, seventy-seven, fell in his home bathroom, hitting his head and ending his life in May 2017.

A source close to Thiel told me, however, that this was never even close to a real opportunity that Thiel would have entertained, largely because Thiel didn't think Ailes would have been a good business partner, based on an introductory business meeting they had several years ago.

Wolff also describes White House senior adviser Stephen Miller, a key influence on Trump's immigration policy positions, as if he has an extra chromosome. "He was supposed to be a speechwriter, but if so, he seemed restricted to bullet points and unable to construct sentences," Wolff wrote. "He was supposed to be a policy adviser but knew little about policy. He was supposed to be the house intellectual but was militantly unread." This description of Miller comes from Wolff, who can barely structure a sentence without at least 18 commas.

Anyone seeking proof (which very obviously excludes Wolff) that Miller is strikingly smart should watch the very entertaining press briefing he led on August 2, 2017. During that briefing, Miller spoke on behalf of the administration backing a bill that aimed to sharply reduce immigration and put a priority on admitting foreigners who know English and have higher work skills.

Miller won the argument against reporters attempting to find something wrong with a bill that follows the same simple logic as one and one is two; when it rains, the ground gets wet; and if it's written by *The Washington Post*'s Dana Milbank, it's stupid.

CNN correspondent Jim Acosta came out of the briefing declaring that Miller "exploded before our eyes" because he "couldn't take that kind of heat."[18]

Here's an example of "that kind of heat," featuring Acosta: "What the president is proposing here does not sound like it's in keeping with American tradition when it comes to immigration," Acosta said to Miller. "The Statue of Liberty says—"

We'll stop there to reflect on a reporter citing a poem on a statue to argue whether a new policy is "in keeping with American tradition." There's an actual document called the Constitution that governs the country, but Acosta saw fit to recite a poem in a policy debate.

"The Statue of Liberty says, 'Give me your tired, your poor, your huddled masses yearning to breathe free,'" said Acosta. "It doesn't say anything about speaking English or being able to be a computer programmer."

Miller responded to Acosta that "the history of immigration, it's actually ebbed and flowed," a statement based on the fact that the U.S. hasn't always admitted the same number of immigrants.

In 1970, about ten million people in the U.S. were foreign-born. A decade later, four million had been added. After another decade, an additional six million. In 2000, an additional ten million were added. Those are not consistent numbers and there's no reason the trajectory always has to go up instead of down or even flat-lining.[19]

Gallup published a survey in January 2017 showing a majority of Americans, 53 percent, are dissatisfied with the level of immigration into the U.S. The immigration issue was crucial in Trump taking the White House, even as the media failed in halting his campaign by calling it racist.[20]

Noting Wolff's description of Miller as a caveman, *Politico*'s White House reporter Eliana Johnson remarked on Twitter that there's "plenty of room to disagree with his views and conclusions, but Stephen Miller can write and Stephen Miller knows immigration policy."[21]

* * *

It's not new for the media to question Trump's sanity or mental acuity.

David Brooks uses his *New York Times* column to do it twice per week and MSNBC's *Morning Joe* does it for three hours daily.

Until Wolff's book came along, serious people outside of the media wouldn't even touch the subject because of how stupid it is.

But *Morning Joe* regular Mike Barnicle in June 2017 asked Democratic House Minority Leader Nancy Pelosi, "Are you concerned about the president's health?"[22]

After a three-second blank stare that would have made Medusa swerve, Pelosi responded, "It's about the facts and the law and there's nothing else."

Unsatisfied with what was a clear choice by Pelosi to avoid a mindless question, well-known journalist Mark Halperin (relegated to obscurity after allegations of sexual harassment surfaced) asked Pelosi, "Are you concerned about his health or not?"

Pelosi would only offer that she was "concerned about [Trump's] fitness for office," the kind of bland phrase Democrats and Republicans use about each other all the time. Conservatives who hate Pelosi might give her a Lifetime Achievement award for her upstanding sanity in the face of stupidity. But she can't be on the show daily to respond each time one of the hosts or panelists turns into a psychiatrist in order to evaluate the president's mental stability.

The previous day on *Morning Joe*, co-host Mika Brzezinski said, "it's possible" Trump is 'mentally ill' and that "at the very least, he's not well."[23]

Joe Scarborough tweeted that Trump is "not well" twice in May.[24,25]

A year earlier, during the 2016 campaign, Brooks, who is not a psychologist, therapist, or psychiatrist, diagnosed Trump with narcissism and wondered whether the then-GOP candidate suggested Trump was "slipping off the rails."[26] He wrote of Trump: "This is a unique moment in American political history in which the mental stability of one of the major party nominees is the dominating subject of conversation." He went on to call Trump a narcissist again.

The dumb questions about whether Trump is retarded are old, but because of Wolff's book, they became new (again). Basic logic and cursory Google searches on the claims in Wolff's book, however, should have rendered those questions null and void.

Wolff suggests in his book that Trump couldn't recognize longtime acquaintances. In one anecdote, he quotes the late Roger Ailes recommending former House Speaker John Boehner as a potential chief of staff for the White House.

"Who's that?" Trump asked, according to Wolff.

Unless Trump simply didn't understand what Ailes had said, there's no reason anyone should believe he didn't know who Boehner is. In 2016, Boehner said that he and Trump frequently golfed and were "texting buddies."[27] In 2013, when Boehner was still speaker, Trump told the *National Review* that he liked Boehner and, "I think he's got a very, very tough job, because he's got factions within his own party that are pretty diametrically opposed to each other, but I think he's got the right temperament, and I think he's a terrific guy."[28]

Trump and Boehner very obviously have a personal history and it's public. But Wolff needed to make Trump look stupid to tantalize readers and some willing media outlets. *New York Magazine* was the first to publish Wolff's claim about Boehner in an excerpt of *Fire and Fury*.[29]

Other parts of Wolff's book cast the president as even more deeply debilitated. "What was, to many of the people who knew Trump well, much more confounding was that he had managed to win this election and arrive at this ultimate accomplishment wholly lacking what in some obvious sense must be the main requirement of the job, what neuroscientists would call executive function," Wolff wrote. "He had somehow won the race for president, but his brain seemed incapable of performing what would be essential tasks in his new job."

President Trump is on TV and in newspapers more than any human on earth, and yet Wolff, based on his time gossiping, had convinced the national media that grandpa got away and is now drooling in the Oval Office. *Fire and Fury* describes a person who repeats and rambles, doesn't recognize reality, and is effectively illiterate. (Reminder: The book is about Trump, not Al Sharpton's attempts to read a teleprompter.)

In the book, Trump has an impossibly short attention span, refuses to learn from policy briefs, and fails to grasp the fundamentals of U.S. government. Where was this version of Trump when giving one of his countless interviews, hosting his rallies, or delivering public remarks at any point between 2015 and now?

Yes, Trump mostly spoke extemporaneously during the campaign, often repeating words and themes, a phenomenon otherwise known as speaking aloud without notes. But he's also delivered dozens of speeches off teleprompters, proving he *can* actually read, frequently going off-script to offer commentary, and then returning to the prepared remarks.

During the campaign, from January to September in 2016, he hosted more than four-and-a-half hours of press conferences, compared to Hillary Clinton's thirty-eight minutes' worth.[30] Here's an experiment: Put a truly mentally slow older person, like Maxine Waters, for example, on stage in front of reporters to answer a succession of questions for one hour. Then compare it to the multiple times Trump did it and see who comes out sharpest.

In an interview in December 2015 with NBC's *Today*, anchor Savannah Guthrie asked if "an alleged extramarital affair" with Monica Lewinsky was "fair game" to bring up in his campaign with regards to Hillary Clinton and her husband's sticky White House misdeeds.[31] A typical mealy-mouthed Republican would have shrunk from the question. Instead, Trump challenged the way it was even framed.

"If he's admitted it, you don't have to use the word 'alleged.'" Trump replied. Guthrie conceded the point and Trump said that yes, bringing up Clinton's taking advantage of an intern was "fair game." Go back and watch the interview on YouTube. It is not the display of a rapidly degenerating mind but instead a razor wit and someone intensely engaged in conversation.

As president, Trump frequently approaches the press pool to answer a range of questions, something former President Obama rarely did. Reporters rightly complained that Obama almost never did press conferences. They don't have the same complaint with Trump because even if he doesn't host formal conferences, he routinely approaches reporters on his own to field an array of questions.

I interviewed Trump in July 2016, four days before the start of the Republican National Convention. For nearly fifteen minutes, he answered every question, sometimes with surprising specificity. "I've always been pro-worker because I grew up with workers," he said at one point in the interview. "Workers were my friends, carpenters, and plumbers, and policemen, and, you know, I'd be on a job site where my father would build houses and I'd be working there as a young boy and even when I got out of college or during different times I'd be working there. I got to know the carpenters and the plumbers. I got to know the sheet-rockers and they were my friends and somehow I relate very well to them, I always have."[32]

Do most reporters know what a sheet-rocker is? I still don't.

Trump did stop the interview at certain points, interruptions that you might call "distractions."

One was to answer a separate call from someone named "Larry," whom he asked to call him back later. He also asked me to hold at one point while he watched a cable news segment about the speakers that were lined up for the GOP convention. "We have some great speakers, they're just announcing the speakers now," he said while I held. Then we resumed.

At other times he did use peculiar phrasing, like when he described himself as a "Republican conservative," instead of the more usual "conservative Republican." Or when he referred to the "LBGT community," swapped for the standard "LGBT." But that a seventy-year-old white, heterosexual male got even the letters right at all should have inspired *Salon.com* to endorse him.

So outlandish are the scenes in Wolff's book that NBC's *Saturday Night Live* perfectly captured the absurdity in an eight-minute sketch so mocking that anyone would believe it.

"Is there anything that you didn't include?" Kate McKinnon, playing MSNBC *Morning Joe* co-host Mika Brzezinski, asks Fred Armisen, playing Wolff.[33]

"Well, sure, probably the worst one is the baby races," replies Armisen.

"What?" asks an exasperated McKinnon.

"There were baby races," Armisen says. "Trump would ask to have two babies placed in his office, usually of different ethnicities. Someone would put a bowl of Goldfish crackers on the other side of the room and Trump would say, 'A thousand bucks on the black one.'"

A bewildered McKinnon asks, "Is that real?!"

With a shrug to suggest it doesn't matter, Armisen replies, "Yeah."

Armisen is then asked if he takes responsibility for errors documented in the book. "Look, you read it right?" he says. "And you liked it? You had fun? Well, what's the problem? You got the gist, so shut up."

He adds, "Now, even the stuff that's not true—it's true."

That's precisely the attitude that the media at-large took toward Wolff's book.

Wolff says Trump is mentally diminished and reporters believed it, despite what we've all seen with our own eyes over the course of two years. But they didn't believe it because they knew it was true. They believed it because they needed it to be.

CHAPTER 4
WOLFF'S WARM-UP ACT: THE HYSTERICAL NATIONAL MEDIA

The media created an environment overripe for a book that smells just like Wolff's.

It's not a matter of whether the national press can report accurate information. It's that the record shows reporters are relentless in assuming the worst about President Trump.

So much so that it's ruining their work.

The day of Trump's inauguration, then-*TIME* magazine reporter Zeke Miller relayed false information to a reporter for *The Dallas Morning News*, which then dispatched a brief for the entire Washington press corps: Miller had told the reporter that a Martin Luther King, Jr., bust had been removed from the Oval Office.[34]

That a statue had been removed from the White House wouldn't be significant if not for our stupid media and the symbolism of a civil rights icon being swept aside by a president who had spent the last year being called a racist by... *The Media*!

For more than an hour the false rumor was blazing across social media, where journalists live, breathe, and build narratives off each other all day.

Finally, the local Texas reporter sent out a correction: "The MLK bust remains in the Oval Office, in addition to the [Winston] Churchill bust, per a [White House] aide. It was apparently obscured by a door and an agent during the spray."[35]

By the way, who even knew there was an MLK bust in the Oval Office? Outside of Washington liberals, the answer is likely close to no one. So, on Inauguration Day, a reporter relays false, racially charged information to another reporter, who then blasts it out to the nation. And all because that first reporter didn't bother to look behind a door.

TIME then had to issue its own correction and its editor, Nancy Gibbs, wrote a "note to our readers" explaining Miller's blunder, even while excusing him for the massive error because he had apologized.[36]

In another case to paint Trump as a disrespectful, uncultured idiot, a media meme was born in November 2017 when the president visited Japanese Prime Minister Shinzo Abe and the two ceremoniously fed the fish in a koi pond.

The two initially flicked spoonsful of food into the pond before Abe, the host, flung the rest of it from his box all at once. Trump followed Abe's lead, emptying the rest of his own box in the pond.

Reporters shared video clips of the encounter on social media that appeared to show just Trump crassly and carelessly dumping the contents of his box in the water.

An article on CNN's website (a place known for its hilarious "facts first" branding) is even now still headlined: "Trump feeds fish, winds up pouring entire box of food into koi pond."[37]

The article begins, "President Donald Trump took a moment out of his whirlwind Japanese trip to connect with nature and feed some fish, but after a few delicate scoops, he resorted to a grand gesture met with some laughter."

Nowhere does it say that Abe was the one to throw his box of fish food into the pond first.

Yashar Ali, who contributes to *New York Magazine* and *The Huffington Post* tweeted the video clip with the comment, "Trump was supposed to feed the koi by the spoonful with PM Abe but quickly got impatient and dumped the whole box of food into the pond."

Ali later deleted the erroneous tweet and admitted his error, but why does this have to keep happening over the dumbest issues? A statue removed from the White House (it wasn't), or Trump disrespecting a ceremony in Japan (he didn't).

So prolific was the inaccurate portrayal of events that the fact-checking website *PolitiFact*, which almost exclusively fact-checks Republicans, wrote up a remarkably honest explainer.

"It was a story that seemed to reinforce stereotypes of President Donald Trump: On a visit to Japan, he was handed a box of food for a ritual feeding of carp, and after doling out a few spoons' worth, he got impatient and dumped the rest of the box all at once," the article said, adding, "One problem: Trump didn't just decide to dump his food on his own. Video shows he was following the lead of his host at the koi pond event, Japanese Prime Minister Shinzo Abe."[38]

You can find examples like these going back to the campaign, when the media spread the lie that Trump mocked the physical disabilities of reporter Serge Kovaleski, whose impairment has crippled his limbs.

As everyone recalls during a rally in late 2015, Trump accused Kovaleski of *The New York Times* of backtracking on his own reporting. Trump had previously cited past work by Kovaleski to back up a claim that Muslims were seen in New Jersey cheering for the September 11 attacks. There remains no strong evidence that any large number of people were seen doing that, but Kovaleski had included the rumor that it happened in a report he authored years previous when he was a journalist at *The Washington Post*.[39]

Trump referred to Kovaleski's backtracking saying, "[The report was] written by a nice guy; now, the poor guy, you got to see this guy…" Trump then started jerking his arms around and, in a mocking tone, said, "Ah, I don't know what I said! Ah, I don't remember!"

If Trump's purpose was to physically imitate Kovaleski, anyone watching would have never known it; and not just because no one would even know who Kovaleski is, if the media hadn't manufactured a controversy in the first place.

Still, actress Meryl Streep (who plays herself in every movie, as once mocked by *Saturday Night Live*, but somehow maintains a reputation as a wide-ranging and talented actress) won accolades from the press for condemning Trump's comments about Kovaleski.

"[T]here was one performance this year that stunned me," she said at the Golden Globes in 2017.

She went on later, "It was that moment when the person asking to sit in the most respected seat in our country imitated a disabled reporter." In her speech, Streep said Trump had mocked Kovaleski for his impairment. "Someone [that Trump] outranked in privilege, power and the capacity to fight back," she said. "It kind of broke my heart when I saw it, and I still can't get it out of my head because it wasn't in a movie. It was real life."

Trump responded by calling Streep a "Hillary lover" and "overrated."

The Washington Post columnist Eugene Robinson said Streep's speech "took a two-by-four to Trump's fragile ego."[40]

"The incident to which [Streep] referred actually took place… when candidate Trump mocked *New York Times* reporter Serge Kovaleski, who has a medical condition that limits the motion of his arms," Robinson said. "While denouncing Kovaleski, whom I have known for years, Trump gestured similarly to the way the reporter does."

The Daily Beast lauded Streep's "riveting" speech, citing her attack on Trump for "callously mock-imitat[ing]" Kovaleski.[41] And Roger Cohen at *The New York Times* rained approval on Streep for having "singled out [Trump's] cruelty, as expressed in Trump's mocking imitation during the campaign of a reporter with a disability."[42]

The media would have everyone believe Kovaleski has Parkinson's disease or at least Restless Leg Syndrome. As it turns out, the power of the internet allows anyone interested to search "Serge Kovaleski" on YouTube and see videos of the reporter.[43] You'll notice he doesn't jerk his arms around, because his mobility is limited. He's still. A corpse would be doing a more accurate imitation than Trump flailing his arms around.

In fact, Trump has used the same effects as he did for Kovaleski when mocking bank executives, Ted Cruz, and responses by former president Obama's generals to questions about fighting the Islamic State.[44] But you don't read about those in the national papers or on cable news. You have to find those on YouTube.

In some cases, journalists and pundits reflexively oppose whatever Trump says, even if it pits them against America. Speaking from the White House Rose Garden in June 2017, Trump said he was withdrawing from the Paris Climate Agreement because it put American workers at an economic disadvantage to the benefit of other countries. "I was elected to represent the citizens of Pittsburgh, not Paris," he said.

He said that the agreement functioned in a way that's "less about the climate and more about other countries gaining a financial advantage over the United States." He called it "a massive redistribution of [the] United States' wealth to other countries" and said that it "handicaps the United States economy" in order to win praise from the very foreign capitals and global activists that have long sought to gain wealth at our country's expense.

That was true. The Paris agreement set up a "Green Climate Fund" wherein more developed nations contributed billions of dollars, which was then to be sent to other countries to pay for "clean energy" and water projects. Under President Obama, the U.S. contributed three billion dollars, more than any other nation. Japan gave the second-most, half of what the U.S. gave. The United Kingdom donated 1.2 billion dollars.[45] France gave a pathetic one billion dollars, a third of what the U.S. gave, and yet the project was named after France's capital! If we're going to give the most money shouldn't we at least get to call it something like "The Fuck-Yeah U.S.A. Pact!?"

"They don't put America first," Trump said of foreign nations (otherwise known as America's competitors). "I do, and I always will."

For anyone with an ounce of patriotism in their blood, those are the words of someone who believes his country and its people are exceptional and shouldn't be burdened to the benefit of others aspiring for the same. But the news media, in an unusual departure from its typical cheery outlook, heard only darkness.

"On a sunny day in the Rose Garden, what could be defined and construed as a dark speech," said MSNBC's Brian Williams, channeling the spirit of a preteen poet immediately at the conclusion of Trump's speech. Admittedly, Williams may have simply been misremembering the true version of events—he has a history of that.

Williams then brought in Nicolle Wallace, a Republican who nonetheless manages day-in and day-out to repeat the same things every other MSNBC host says. "It was an incredibly cynical look at our role in the world," she said, later calling it "one of the most bleak depictions of America's role in the world."

Fareed Zakaria on CNN said, "I think...this will be the day that the United States resigned as the leader of the free world."[46]

Where is it written that for the U.S. to lead the world it must first crush its productive workforce then follow up by giving billions to its competitors? Yet the theme stuck on repeat was that Trump had wrecked American "leadership."

A *Washington Post* editorial said Trump "dealt a blow to the U.S. leadership that has helped promote peace and prosperity for the past seven decades under Republican and Democratic presidents alike. Under their guidance, the United States acted with selflessness and enlightened self-interest."[47] It may also be "enlightened" to stop cutting down trees and turning them into near-obsolete newspapers, but presumably the *Post* wouldn't be so interested in "selflessness" then.

Back on MSNBC, would-be marketing expert Donny Deutsche attempted to define the appropriate way to lead. "Even if we are contributing more in many instances than the rest of the world," he said, "that's what leaders do."[48] No, that's what nuns do. American presidents look out for U.S. interests. A theory at least in exercise in this case.

The Paris deal boiled down to nearly 200 countries setting up their own individual rules to curb carbon emission. That included countries, like India, receiving billions in foreign aid from more developed economies and other countries, like China, doing less to curb emissions and at a slower pace to fulfill their own end of the agreement.[49]

It's true that there were no enforcement mechanisms to ensure each country met its obligation, and Trump repeatedly said he was willing to re-enter the same or a similar deal under different terms for the U.S., but any time he asserts the country's right to put itself first, the media winces as if they just got a text alert from Anthony Weiner.

The press said Trump's speech was dark. Everyone else said: *For who?!*

The next month, the president delivered a moving speech in Poland championing the spread of Western democracy and calling on European nations to defend their sovereignty. He complimented America's allies while calling on Russia to "cease its destabilizing activities in Ukraine and elsewhere and its support for hostile regimes."

Trump said the U.S. "will always welcome new citizens who share our values and love our people" but that "our borders will always be closed to terrorism and extremism of any kind." Any sane person might hear those words and call it at least an OK speech, but because the subject doesn't relate to Russia stealing the election from Hillary Clinton or to an erosion of press freedom by way of Trump tweeting insults at cable news, the media are left sputtering for novel ways to hate the president.

The Washington Post's news article on Trump's speech described it as "a dark and provocative address with nationalist overtones."[50] "Nationalist" is the media's dismissive catch-all term for any policy that defines America as an independent country.

On the *Post*'s opinion page, liberal columnist Eugene Robinson took the portion of Trump's speech about sovereignty as an assault on his favorite ethnic foods. "Imagine Italy without tomato sauce, a gift from the New World," Robinson wrote in earnest on what is no doubt a keyboard smudged with marinara.[51]

Robinson's *Post* colleague Jonathan Capehart summed up Trump's speech as a mash-up of "white-nationalist dog whistles."[52]

During a portion of Trump's remarks, he said of Western civilization, "We write symphonies. We pursue innovation. We celebrate our ancient heroes, embrace our timeless traditions and customs, and always seek to explore and discover brand-new frontiers."

Capehart called the line about symphonies "a familiar boast that swells the chests of white nationalists everywhere."

In what world?

It's easy to imagine any attempt at engaging Capehart in polite small talk invariably leading to deeply uncomfortable lectures about micro-aggressions.

How's the weather?

Capehart: *Check your privilege!*

At the news website *Vox*, foreign policy writer Sarah Wildman dubbed Trump's speech "an alt-right manifesto" with "the type of dire, last-chance wording often utilized by the far right."[53]

In May 2017, North Korea warned of "complete destruction" of the U.S. and "the lives of hundreds of millions of Americans" but Waldman found it "dire" when Trump, in his Poland speech, said, "The fundamental question of our time is whether the West has the will to survive."[54]

Journalists on social media were also quick to pass around a video clip of Poland's first lady Agata Kornhauser-Duda shaking Melania Trump's hand before the president's, who had stuck his own hand out. Several news websites described it as if the Polish first lady had spit on her own hand before walking away.

Vanity Fair's since-updated article was and remains headlined, "The First Lady of Poland Smoothly Avoided Shaking Donald Trump's Hand."[55]

CNN political analyst Chris Cillizza, who I believe is supposed to be an adult male, reacted to the non-incident by tweeting, "OHMYGODOHMYGODOHMYGOD..."[56]

The longer video clip, however, showed Kornhauser-Duda simply returning to the president after having greeted Melania. Almost like anyone might do in a normal, if slightly clumsy welcoming.

The hatred for Trump burns so hot in the media journalists will instantly defend an enemy to the U.S. if it keeps them consistent in their opposition to everything he does. That's not hyperbole for the sake of making a point. This has literally happened.

In September 2017, Trump said at the United Nations General Assembly that America would crush North Korea should Kim Jong-un attack the U.S. or our allies. Reporters and commentators reacted as if he had just threatened Switzerland on a whim.

Trump had simply said that the U.S. "has great strength and patience, but if it is forced to defend itself or its allies, we will have no choice but to totally destroy North Korea," a relatively measured response to years of hostility from Kim's regime.

But an emotionally wrecked Nicholas Kristof wrote in *The New York Times* that, "There were gasps in the hall: A forum for peace was used to threaten to annihilate a nation of 25 million people."[57] His colleague Gail Collins said the "big takeaway" of Trump's address to the UN was "that the president of the United States had threatened to destroy a country with twenty-five million people."[58] *USA Today* called Trump's remarks "rancorous" and "tabloid bombast."[59]

It's as if up until January 20, 2017, Kim had been sending America Christmas cards and the national media needed to know why the new president was being so bitchy. Just in 2016, North Korea threatened to blow up Manhattan with a hydrogen bomb, reduce the U.S. to "flames and ashes," and announced that it was close to launching a "pre-emptive" nuclear attack. If there were just one area of agreement between the media and Trump, it should be that Kim is a lunatic, former President Barack Obama's "strategic patience" failed, and it's time to try something new.

Trump is trying something new.

Yet, ABC anchor Terry Moran said Trump's vow to retaliate "borders on the threat of committing a war crime," the kind of comment that would normally be used by conservatives to parody MSNBC's primetime hosts.[60] Except a parody is meant to be an exaggeration and MSNBC's Lawrence O'Donnell literally said the same thing as Moran. "At UN Trump threatened to commit a war crime," O'Donnell tweeted after Trump's speech.[61]

Jessica Schulberg, a reporter for the liberal *Huffington Post*, even suggested that Trump's comments justify North Korea's provocations. Reacting to Trump's speech on Twitter, she wrote in sarcasm, "Gee, Kim Jon-un is so irrational for wanting nuclear weapons."[62]

Kim starves his own people and the media are siding with him over them and, more importantly, over us.

Kim responded to Trump's remarks through North Korea's state media, calling the president a "mentally deranged U.S. dotard," adding that he would make Trump "pay dearly for his speech."

The mostly forgotten Chelsea Handler said on Twitter that the response was "a little bit more sane" than Trump, then asked if the U.S. and Korea could "trade" leaders.[63]

North Korea is quickly advancing its capability to reach any major U.S. city with a missile carrying a nuclear bomb, something Trump said in January "won't happen!"

It's happening, and now it's them or us.

At least we know which side the media are on. This is the atmosphere our national press has created. It's against Trump and what his voters wanted to the point of hysteria. The opportunity was wide open for a book like *Fire and Fury*, thanks to the news media.

Wolff took full advantage.

CHAPTER 5

MEDIA ASK WOLFF, "MAY I CARRY THIS BULLSHIT FOR YOU?"

It amounts to media malpractice that would-be respectable news outlets publicized the unsanitary content in Wolff's book.

The Guardian, a British-based publication, was in safe territory publishing the first bits from *Fire and Fury*, which mostly center on an interview Wolff conducted with Steve Bannon, who served for a while as the White House political strategist.

The interview was apparently on the record, a nonsensical move by Bannon, who afterward apologized for his remarks. Regardless, the interview was real, and Bannon never denied talking to Wolff. "They're going to crack Don Junior like an egg on national TV," Bannon said, according to the book, referring to Trump's son Donald Trump Jr. having met with a Russian lawyer during the campaign.[64]

That meeting has been a focus of special counsel Robert Mueller's investigation into Russia's interference in the 2016 election, and whether that included collusion with the Trump campaign. "Even if you thought that this was not treasonous, or unpatriotic, or bad shit, and I happen to think it's all of that, you should have called the FBI immediately," Bannon said of the meeting.

Crucial context to this is that Bannon is, if only slightly, a weird person.

As head of the *Breitbart News* website, Bannon ensured that the site consistently backed Trump's agenda. He joined Trump's campaign as chairman in late 2016, lasted through the election, and then joined the White House. But while there, he was very apparently the source of countless leaks to the press and, in what is probably the biggest, most inexplicable move in the history of politics, he called a liberal magazine (while still employed by the administration) to contradict positions held by the White House. "There's no military solution [to North Korea's nuclear threats], forget it," Bannon said in the interview, though the White House and Trump himself had repeatedly said that everything, including military solutions, were on the table in resolving the North Korea problem.[65]

Bannon went on to rant about China and how he alone was fixing the economic threat the country poses. "I'm changing out people at East Asian Defense; I'm getting hawks in," he told the magazine. "I'm getting Susan Thornton [the acting head of East Asian and Pacific Affairs] out at State."

This is how low-level, nobody Capitol Hill staffers, who wish they were important, talk about their obscure congressman boss.

Low-level, nobody Hill staffer: *Yeah, I get a lot of facetime with the congressman. I'm the one he talks to. I make most of the decisions.*

The low-level, nobody Hill staffer acts like he's changing the world while everyone else listening wonders: *Is he okay? And does he know there's food in his hair?*

Admittedly, it's somewhat odd, given that Bannon actually was important and didn't need to talk this way. But he did.

Bannon was removed from his White House job two days after the interview published.

That a White House official was speaking this way to any journalist should be cause for alarm, and Bannon's interview with Wolff rightfully made news. Though Bannon's comments were fair in news value, almost everything outside of that was inaccurate and inconsistent with reality or recklessly disregarded the obvious truth.

The Hollywood Reporter, where Wolff is a columnist, printed excerpts from Wolff's book, including a portion where Murdoch allegedly hangs up the phone after a call with Trump and says of the new president, "What a fucking moron."[66]

In the actual book, the quote appears as, "What a fucking idiot."

Something was either lost in translation between the book and the column or, more likely, it was a small but glaring example of Wolff's looseness and carelessness with accuracy reflected in a sloppy copy-and-paste job.

Wolff wrote that it was Trump's tweet in July 2017 announcing John Kelly as his new chief of staff that informed the retired general he would be moving from the Department of Homeland Security, where he had been the director, to manage the West Wing.

"In fact, Kelly—who would soon abjectly apologize to [outgoing Chief of Staff Reince] Priebus for the basic lack of courtesy in the way his dismissal was handled—had not been consulted about his appointment," Wolff wrote in the book. "The president's tweet was the first he knew of it."

But *The New York Times* reported at the time of the announcement that Trump had "offered the job to Mr. Kelly a few days" before the tweet.[67]

Do we believe the fantastical account in Kelly's book that Trump made an announcement about the most important job in the White House on Twitter first, or the far more likely scenario that he had consulted Kelly days beforehand?

These should have served as massive warning that perhaps, at the least, *Fire and Fury* wasn't a fully honest portrayal of Trump's White House.

Media: *Nah!*

Here's the kind of grilling Wolff got in a January 8 interview on *CBS This Morning*:

Anchor Jeff Glor: "President Trump yesterday said the book is a fake book. He said you are totally discredited as an author. Is everything in the book true?"

Wolff: "Everything in the book is true."

Glor: "And your response to that?"

Wolff: "Well, I'm waiting for a nickname [from Trump]."

[Glor's co-anchors Gayle King and Norah O'Donnell laugh off camera.]

Glor: "You don't have one yet?"

Wolff: "Where's my nickname?"

That's the aggressive follow-up I hope conservative authors expect from CBS News when they call the next Democratic president mentally disabled, presuming a conservative book like that would even be featured on network television.

Author Ed Klein, former editor in chief of *The New York Times Magazine*, wrote an equally salacious book about Barack Obama and Hillary Clinton, but coverage of the book was rarely seen outside of Fox News. Klein's 2012 book *The Amateur* was, like *Fire and Fury*, a White House insider account that described Obama as thin-skinned, ill-equipped, and vain. It hit number one on the *Times'* bestseller list and stayed there for a month, despite nearly no attention from the mainstream media.[68]

The Amateur included on-record interviews with Reverend Jeremiah Wright, wherein Obama's incendiary longtime pastor claimed that the Obama 2008 campaign had offered him a monetary bribe in exchange for keeping a low profile before the election.

Wow, that's interesting!

But a *New York Times* book review at the time dismissed the revelation, noting that, "any biographical subject has bitter ex-friends and associates." The review called Klein's book "skimpy" and, again, "bitter."[69] Klein wasn't interviewed at all by ABC, CNN, NBC, MSNBC, or CBS. If he had, it's safe to assume Klein would have received more pointed questions than, "Is everything in the book true?"

By contrast, Wolff appeared on:

- NBC's *Today*
- NBC's *Meet the Press*
- ABC's *The View*
- *CBS This Morning*
- HBO's *Real Time with Bill Maher*
- CNBC's *Squawk Box*
- CNBC's *Power Lunch*
- MSNBC's *Morning Joe*
- MSNBC's *Morning Joe* (a second time)
- MSNBC's *Hardball*
- MSNBC's *The Last Word*

- CNN's *Tonight*
- CNN's *Smerconish*
- PBS's *News Hour*

The Los Angeles Times' politics and culture columnist Virginia Heffernan made the unfortunate prediction that, because Wolff supposedly had a good editor and his book was fact-checked, the book would "withstand whatever charges of journalistic impropriety come at it."

If there were a penalty for embarrassing yourself with how wrong you can be, the national papers' opinion pages would be empty. (These are the people, by the way, who think it's sassy and daring to call Trump "shameless.") Incidentally, Heffernan's column was ever-so fittingly headlined, "Why believe Michael Wolff? Because, for now, this stuff is too good not to."[70]

In another dumbfounding chapter of the Wolff saga, he admitted in his book that he was basically talking out of his ass when he recounted a private conversation between Tony Blair and Jared Kushner, in which Blair told Trump's son-in-law that UK intelligence may have spied on the Trump campaign and Trump himself. "There was, he suggested, the possibility that the British had had the Trump campaign staff under surveillance, monitoring its telephone calls and other communications and possibly even Trump himself," Wolff wrote.

The spying supposedly came at the prodding of the Obama administration.

"So," Wolff continued, "although the Obama administration would not have asked the British to spy on the Trump campaign, the Brits would have been led to understand how helpful it might be if they did."

You can imagine Wolff verbally telling this story, eyes bulging, and hoping his audience remains distracted by his wild fantasy as he swipes their wallets and watches.

Yes, a former British spy, Christopher Steele, did receive money from the Democratic National Committee and the Hillary Clinton campaign via the firm Fusion GPS in order to compile the garbage "dossier" on Trump. Steele, in turn, then paid Russians to tell him bad things about Trump.[71] But that is not the same thing as official British intelligence putting Trump under "surveillance."

Wolff alleges that the conversation between Blair and Kushner took place at the White House in February 2017 because Blair was "seeking to prove his usefulness to this new White House" and "particularly intent on helping shepherd some of Jared's Middle East initiatives."

Mind you, this is Tony Blair, who served as Britain's prime minister for a decade. And yet, Wolff's book pushes the idea that Blair needed to suck up to Kushner, who had no government experience and, by the book's own admission was "more than a little desperate" for advice.

A distinguished former British prime minister is ingratiating himself to Kushner because what? He needs a job? It's laughable.

Here's how Wolff washes his hands of any implication he might have in the hearsay he spread: "It was unclear whether Blair's information was rumor, informed conjecture, his own speculation, or solid stuff."

Translated for the digital age, Wolff means something to the effect of: ˉ_(ツ)_/ˉ

Blair then had to publicly deny the encounter with Kushner, as was detailed by Wolff. "This story is a complete fabrication, literally from beginning to end," he said in an interview on BBC Radio, acknowledging though that he does know Kushner. "I've never had such conversation in the White House, outside of the White House, with Jared Kushner or with anybody else."[72]

And, in a moment of depressing insight perfectly applicable to Wolff's book and its media reception, Blair bemoaned the state of working in public affairs. "The story is a sort of reflection on the crazy state of modern politics," he said. "Here's a story that is literally an invention and is now halfway around the world with conspiracy theories attached to it. That's modern politics."

That's modern politics in the age of Trump.

* * *

When *Fire and Fury* had been out for two weeks and its initial buzz had worn off, Wolff raised the hysteria once again by claiming that seventy-one-year-old Trump was actively and presently engaged in an extramarital affair.

In a January 19 appearance on HBO's *Real Time with Bill Maher*, the show's host asked Wolff to share something from his book that had not yet made news. "There is something in the book that I was absolutely sure of, but it was so incendiary that I just didn't have the ultimate proof," Wolff said.

Asked by Maher if it was related to "a woman thing," Wolff said yes, but that he couldn't say it aloud because he, "didn't have the blue dress."

Jesus Christ.

"Oh, it's somebody he's fucking now?" Maher pressed.

"It is."

Wolff said, however, that "reading between the lines" at a specific point in his book would inspire a "bingo" moment.

Reporters thereafter homed in on a paragraph that occurs late in *Fire and Fury*.

"The president had been spending a notable amount of private time with [UN Ambassador Nikki] Haley on Air Force One and was seen to be grooming her for a national political future," the paragraph said. "Haley, who was much more of a traditional Republican, one with a pronounced moderate streak—a type increasingly known as a Jarvanka Republican—was, evident to many, being mentioned in Trump ways." (As an aside, I live in Washington, and I can promise you no one is using the term "Jarvanka Republican.")

The book further stated that Haley "had concluded that Trump's tenure would last, at best, a single term, and that she, with the requisite submission, could be his heir apparent."

Serious journalists at least acknowledged the volume of mucous it must have required for Wolff to spread that rumor around with no proof. But Wolff's credibility had already been bolstered by the book's fanatical media coverage up to that point.

The affair story was picked up by *People* magazine[73], *Vanity Fair*[74], and *Entertainment Weekly*[75].

In a podcast interview, the news website *Politico* asked Haley to respond to the allegation.[76] She denied it and said up to that point she had "literally been on Air Force One once and there were several people in the room when I was there."

But in yet another interview with the women's lifestyle publication *theSkimm*, Wolff clung to his fabrication. Asked about Haley's denial of the rumor, Wolff said, "I would say she seems to have embraced it."[77] He continued, "Well, I don't know. All she does is hammer on this fact. I mean, if I were being accused of something—and I am not accusing her of anything. She hasn't tried to avoid this, let's say."

Other than condemning the 2018 Grammys for allowing different celebrities (and Hillary Clinton) to read excerpts of the book as a joke during the Awards Ceremony, Haley's comments to *Politico* were the only time she addressed the book at all, let alone the dumb and obviously untrue rumor. She never "embraced" anything, which was really just another way for Wolff to say, "she wanted it."

On his media tour, Wolff would often make a sick claim—like the president is retarded, for example—and then cover himself by attributing it to his "sources" and "reporting."

Yet Wolff accused Haley of having the affair.

In his interview with Bill Maher, the host asked if the so-far unnoticed bit in his book was "a woman thing" and if it was related to somebody Trump is "fucking now."

Wolff simply replied, "It is" and that it was something he was "absolutely sure of."

The affair was a claim made directly by him, though he subsequently attempted to skirt responsibility for it by attributing the rumor to more "sources." At this point, Wolff had already served his purpose anyway, inflicting maximum damage on Trump's presidency, and so the media were ready to dump him and take the moral high ground.

Elise Jordan, who regularly participates in the three hours of Trump hate known as *Morning Joe*, tweeted, "No, Michael Wolff, it was not fun for Nikki Haley to have to deny the sexist and unfounded rumors you floated that she was having an affair with her boss, the President of the United States."[78]

"This is so vile," tweeted CNN anchor Jake Tapper in response to Wolff's comments to *theSkimm*.[79]

Jonathan Swan, a well-known reporter for *Axios* in Washington, said in a tweet to Wolff that the author should remove his name from forthcoming editions of the book: "Hey @MichaelWolffNYC: it must be fun to write and say whatever you want under the banner of 'non-fiction,' with zero fact-checking or basic decency…I have no idea why you put me in your author acknowledgments but please remove my name for the next edition."[80]

Swan, among other journalists, is listed in the acknowledgments under "many friends, colleagues and generous people in the greater media and political world [who] have made this a smarter book."

Swan, however, did not help Wolff with his book.

The errors, lies, and unsupported claims in Wolff's book are legion, from the botched copy-and-paste jobs to the explicit slander. Yet a complicit media, eager to alienate Trump even further from the public, lent Wolff their credibility, aiding *Fire and Fury* to inflict untold damage to the presidency.

The press' conscience may have made an occasional appearance covering Wolff's book, but it was after it was too late. Wolff had made his name, and the White House had been buried by the coverage.

CHAPTER 6

MORNING JOE GIVES WOLFF'S CREDIBILITY A FACELIFT

No media entity encapsulates the stupidity and the rise and fall of Wolff's book like MSNBC's *Morning Joe*.

Trump and the show's perpetually squinty co-hosts, Mika Brzezinski and Joe Scarborough, share a personal history that Trump benefitted from during the 2016 Republican primary. He was frequently invited to talk at length and the show's hosts and panelists showered praise on him for shredding the fourteen other serious GOP candidates.

Things turned south, however, during the general election when *Morning Joe*'s coverage of Trump became increasingly negative (as many of the conservative geeks on Twitter, to their credit, predicted). The tension climaxed on June 29 when Trump tweeted seemingly out of nowhere that morning that he had seen "low-I.Q. crazy" Brzezinski around the 2017 new year "bleeding badly from a face-lift."

In ferocious anti-Trump mode for more than a year, *Morning Joe* was among the first news programs to back Wolff on his book and put its weighty credibility with all of Washington, DC, media behind it, even though Wolff's credibility as a journalist has hung on a thread for years.

In 2004, Michelle Cottle, then a senior editor for the liberal *New Republic*, wrote that details portrayed even in Wolff's columns "aren't recreated so much as created—springing from Wolff's imagination rather than from actual knowledge of events."[81]

But *Morning Joe* was there to clean things up.

"I've got to say, this book rings true on just about everything that I read," Scarborough, a former Republican congressman, said on the January 4 edition of the show before its publication. "Of all the things Mika and I have known about Trump over the past 10, 11 years. What we knew over the last 12 to 24 months, what we knew after we stopped talking to him. Again, I haven't read anything in here…that didn't ring true to me. Everything else does. And it follows everything that all of my sources have been telling me for 12 months now."

Wolff was interviewed on the show four days later, during which Scarborough skated over criticisms of the numerous errors and inaccuracies in the book that had already surfaced on the internet. "But the bigger point is, your critics, they run with these little specific things," said Scarborough, lending a hand in helping Wolff excuse his shoddy work. "But getting a part of a story wrong here or getting something else…but sometimes the sources, yeah, get it a little off."

It's the sources, you see, who sometimes "get it a little off." You can't blame Wolff for them giving him false information as if it were his job to suss that out before it went to print!

Brzezinski polished the book's problems by saying that even if there are a bunch of errors and inconsistencies, "the spirit of it is completely true" and, "This is the Trump I know."

This amounted to an effective endorsement of Wolff's book.

Compounding the stupidity were *Morning Joe*'s own frequent guests—somewhat respected journalists—who would cast a cloud of doubt over Wolff's credibility and regardless fall in line behind Scarborough and Brzezinski to promote the book's content.

"No way to know how much of Wolff's account is fanciful elaboration but even 20 percent being true…America what did you do," *Commentary* magazine editor and frequent *Morning Joe* editor John Podhoretz tweeted on January 3.

On the show, Podhoretz said Wolff is known to play "fast and loose" with the truth and that in his book he "doesn't source himself well, speculation is talked about in exactly the same way that [the] actual facts that he's gathered are talked about. You cannot source out the gossip from the fact. It's very difficult. This is clearly going to be a problem with this book."

After that glowing review of Wolff's professionalism, Podhoretz still said that the author's "portrait" of the White House in chaos seemed true.

NBC's John Heilemann questioned Wolff's "sourcing and methods," then went on to say the book "rings true." He continued, "The array of quotations in the book and the assessments, all consistent of the closest people to the President, working with him, as being essentially a child. That is a devastating portrait and again, I think one, putting aside questions of Michael Wolff as a journalist, that rings true…"

What does Halperin mean, "Putting aside question of Michael Wolff as a journalist"? Isn't Wolff's credibility as a journalist kind of what the entire credibility of his sham book hangs on?

How would Heilemann describe Ted Bundy?

Heilemann: *He was a serial murderer, but putting aside questions of Ted Bundy's basic humanity, he was handsome!*

On January 5, *Morning Joe* invited Janice Min—editor of *The Hollywood Reporter*, where Wolff writes a column—to spend ten minutes backing *Fire and Fury*'s credibility.

By February, Wolff's book had already fallen apart, and he was fully under siege for having suggested, without any evidence, that Nikki Haley was sleeping with Trump.

Yet, there was *Morning Joe* inviting Wolff on to offer analysis about the Russia investigation. "Give us a sense of where you think this is leading, given your reporting in this book," Brzezinski asked Wolff on the February 1 edition of the show.

Wolff was allotted six minutes to reaffirm the findings of his book, helped along by questions like *The Atlantic*'s Jeffrey Goldberg that began, "Based on your understanding…"

Wolff had just spent nearly a month feeding a lie about Trump having dementia, describing the executive branch of government as dangerously chaotic, and suggesting the United Nations Ambassador was having an affair with the president. Here, *Morning Joe* was using him as a White House expert fit to comment on the Russia investigation.

Then in a breakneck mood swing, Brzezinski went on the attack over the Nikki Haley rumor. "The entire credibility of your book… let's put it on this next question: Do you regret inferring anything about Nikki Haley?" she asked Wolff.

Wolff replied by lying, claiming he had never made any accusations and that it was Haley keeping the rumor alive. (By denying the sick charge, it was apparently Haley's fault that people were still talking about it.) So, *Morning Joe* had spent hours boosting Wolff's book, including scheduling him to come on the show twice to talk about it. Suddenly, Brzezinski was ready to put "the entire credibility" on the question of Haley's affair? Interesting how that worked out. After nearly a month of promoting Wolff and his book, he had served his purpose and *Morning Joe* was okay with dumping him.

"Come on, are you kidding?" Brzezinski said to Wolff after he denied he was responsible for pushing the rumor about Haley. "You're on the set of *Morning Joe*. We don't B.S. here….If you don't get it, if you don't get what we're talking about, I'm sorry. This is awkward. You're here on the set with us, but we're done."

After being thrown off the show he was invited on, Wolff tweeted, "My bad, the President is right about Mika." He then accused Scarborough and Brzezinski of having been "eager to gossip about who Trump might be sleeping with" the last time he was on their show. "It really would be hard to gossip more eagerly off camera than Mika and Joe gossip," he said.

That's one claim by Wolff, at least, that might be true.

By the way, Wolff entirely abandoned the Haley affair rumor a few days after being kicked off *Morning Joe*. In a February 22 interview with a Dutch television show, Wolff finally admitted, "I do not know if the president is having an affair." He added, however, "Do I think he is? I think it would be unlikely that he has suddenly become a faithful husband."

This is Wolff's way of saying: Yes, I spread an evidence-free smear and no, I can't back it up, but I'm not ready to get off this ride just yet.

Unfortunately for Wolff, the media no longer needed him.

On February 26, *The Washington Post* media critic Erik Wemple wrote a column under the headline, "Michael Wolff is crumbling before our eyes."[82]

Fine timing.

CHAPTER 7
FIRE AND FURY: EMBARRASSING AND SLOPPY

Setting aside even the most scandalized claims in Wolff's book, how brazenly stupid he was in failing to get basic facts right should have rendered him fully unemployable for the rest of his career in journalism. Numbers, identifiers, and specific events that are easily verifiable are wrong throughout *Fire and Fury*.

In one scene, Wolff describes a February 2017 breakfast meeting at the Four Seasons in Washington, DC, attended by Ivanka Trump, senior lawmakers, business executives, and "labor secretary nominee Wilbur Ross."

Wilbur Ross was nominated as Secretary of Commerce, not Labor.

Wolff also said that *Washington Post* reporter Mark Berman was there, though Berman has since said he has never been to the hotel's restaurant. (Berman later said that Wolff had admitted to mixing up his name for Mike Berman, a prominent Democratic lawyer in Washington.)[83]

Early in the book, Wolff got former White House Communications Director Hope Hicks' age wrong by two years. Toward the end, he says Trump tried to set up a meeting in August with Mitch McConnell, only to have the senator's staff decline because it would have conflicted with a haircut appointment. *Washington Post* reporter Ashley Parker said that bit of bitchy gossip was known well by many reporters but that none could confirm it with anyone who would truly know, so they never printed it. Every reporter who checked their sources couldn't get legitimate corroboration of the rumor. Naturally, it would end up in Wolff's book, next to every other annoying and wrong piece.

Jonathan Swan, a respected reporter in Washington, said it was a "disgrace" for Wolff to have printed the story, given its lack of evidence.[84]

This goes on and on and on.

In a chapter on the massive annual conservative CPAC gathering, where in 2011 Trump gave his first major political speech, Wolff appears to just have completely fabricated the details. "In 2011," Wolff wrote, "professing conservative fealty, Trump lobbied the group for a speaking slot and, with reports of a substantial cash contribution, was awarded a fifteen-minute berth."

This is not true.

The author and frequent Fox News guest Lisa De Pasquale, who used to run CPAC as its top director, told me Trump was invited to speak by the now-defunct gay Republican group GOProud, which was a CPAC sponsor (a controversy that was more interesting than most of Wolff's book, if you care to look it up).

Chris Barron, a Republican activist and a cofounder of GOProud, sold De Pasquale on giving Trump a slot. "Basically, he said, 'We can get you Trump,' " she told me. "And I said go for it."

This isn't even inside knowledge.

CNN reported it in March 2016: "Trump came to the nation's capital at the behest of GOProud, a small upstart group of gay conservatives who, in a Hail Mary attempt to make a name for themselves among Republicans, had invited him to be a surprise speaker at the 2011 Conservative Political Action Conference, the nation's largest annual gathering of right-wing activists," the report said.[85]

At the time, Trump was considering a run for the Republican nomination and he used that opportunity to thrust himself into national politics. In a prophetic portion of Trump's CPAC speech, he said: "During my lifetime, I've always been told that a person of great accomplishment and achievement cannot become a politician or run for political office because there are too many enemies, both very smart and not so smart, strewn along this highway to success.

"People who have been in wars—and this is war; life is pleasant, but it can be war—people who have been in wars, even the most successful of them, leave themselves open to great criticism from the many that they have beaten and those that have watched the battles.

"The fact is, this theory of a very successful person running for office is rarely tested because most successful people don't want to be scrutinized or abused. And that's what happens. If you see it, that's what happens. And this is why we don't have the kind of people that we should have running for office. Unfortunately, however, this is the kind of person that the country needs, and they need it now. We don't have time to wait 25 years and get it right…This country is in serious trouble. We need it now."

Wow, in what world would a successful person be so relentlessly ripped apart just by running for president? Oh wait, never mind.

So numerous and shockingly neglectful are the errors in Wolff's book that one of *The Washington Post*'s media critics declared that, "It's not even clear that the book was vetted."

Here we define "vetted" as an editor simply asking Wolff, "Did you Google that one first?"

The answer is clear from reading the book.

CHAPTER 8

TRUMP, THE BOOK SALESMAN

Fire and Fury would have been a niche book targeting the people who eat, sleep, and dream their hatred for Trump (most of them are in the national media), but because Trump cannot resist punching back, even when it means punching down, the president elevated the book.

Over. And over. And over.

In just days, thanks largely to aid from the White House, it had sold a million copies worldwide, an astronomical feat in book publishing today.[86]

Before the book had even been released, the administration gave it publicity you literally cannot buy.

"This book is filled with false and misleading accounts from individuals who have no access or influence with the White House," White House press secretary Sarah Huckabee Sanders said in an official statement. "Participating in a book that can only be described as trashy tabloid fiction exposes their sad desperate attempts at relevancy."

That was just the start of something truly beautiful for a book that would have otherwise tickled some liberals and been forgotten about by the rest of us.

Because Wolff claimed in his book that the first lady had not supported Trump's run for president, and that she wept when the results made him the winner on Election Day, the East Wing came out with its own statement: "The book is clearly going to be sold in the bargain fiction section," said Stephanie Grisham, communications director for the first lady. "Mrs. Trump supported her husband's decision to run for President and in fact, encouraged him to do so. She was confident he would win and was very happy when he did."

That's two official White House statements elevating a book they wanted people to ignore. What's the opposite of: Good idea, bro?

Then Trump's attorney issued a letter to the publisher threatening to sue for defamation, a case no serious First Amendment lawyer would ever expect to win.[87]

Ecstatic, the publisher moved up the book's release date a full four days.[88]

And life would not be complete if Trump didn't tweet about those who slight him from the depths of the sewer: "I authorized zero access to White House (actually turned him down many times) for author of phony book!" he tweeted on January 4, keeping interesting the book alive and well. "I never spoke to him for book. Full of lies, misrepresentations and sources that don't exist. Look at this guy's past and watch what happens to him and Sloppy Steve!"

That was just the first one. It went on for days.

January 5: "Well, now that collusion with Russia is proving to be a total hoax and the only collusion is with Hillary Clinton and the FBI/Russia, the Fake News Media (Mainstream) and this phony new book are hitting out at every new front imaginable. They should try winning an election. Sad!"

January 5: "Michael Wolff is a total loser who made up stories in order to sell this really boring and untruthful book. He used Sloppy Steve Bannon, who cried when he got fired and begged for his job. Now Sloppy Steve has been dumped like a dog by almost everyone. Too bad!"

January 6 (after the media took the book's bait on Trump's mental health): "Now that Russian collusion, after one year of intense study, has proven to be a total hoax on the American public, the Democrats and their lapdogs, the Fake News Mainstream Media, are taking out the old Ronald Reagan playbook and screaming mental stability and intelligence…actually, throughout my life, my two greatest assets have been mental stability and being, like, really smart. Crooked Hillary Clinton also played these cards very hard and, as everyone knows, went down in flames. I went from VERY successful businessman, to top T.V. Star…to President of the United States (on my first try). I think that would qualify as not smart, but genius… and a very stable genius at that!"

On the same day as this tweet, Trump emerged from a meeting with congressional Republicans at Camp David to give a statement on legislative priorities and then take questions from the press (i.e., give more free publicity) to *Fire and Fury*. One reporter asked Trump why, given he had a day dedicated to policy discussion, he had sent a tweet out that morning about his mental stability.

Trump then might as well have spent the next two minutes with a sign on his bare ass that said: "*Buy* Fire and Fury! *In Bookstores Everywhere! Selling Like Big Hot Cakes! Get It While You Can!*"

Instead, here's Trump's answer: "Well, only because I went to the best colleges for college...I had a situation where I was a very excellent student. Came out and made billions and billions of dollars. Became one of the top businesspeople. Went to television and, for ten years, was a tremendous success, as you probably have heard. Ran for President one time and won.

"And then I hear this guy that does not know me, doesn't know me at all. By the way, did not interview me...he said he interviewed me for three hours in the White House. It didn't exist, okay? It's in his imagination.

"And what I was heartened by—because I talk about fake news and the fake news media—was the fact that so many of the people that I talk about, in terms of fake news, actually came to the defense of this great administration and even myself because they know the author and they know he's a fraud.

"And...look at some of his past books. He did a book on Rupert Murdoch. It was a terrible exposé and it was false. So much of it was false. I consider it a work of fiction and I think it's a disgrace that somebody is able to have something, do something like that. The libel laws are very weak in this country. If they were strong, it would be very helpful. You wouldn't have things like that happen where you can say whatever comes to your head.

"But, just so you know, I never interviewed with him in the White House at all. He was never in the Oval Office. We didn't have an interview. And I did a quick interview with him a long time ago having to do with an article, but I don't know this man. I guess sloppy Steve brought him into the White House quite a bit, and it was one of those things. That's why sloppy Steve is now looking for a job."

Following two official White House statements, two tweets to his 48 million followers, a press conference, and a lawsuit threat, Trump had said his piece and finally put it to rest.

Just kidding! The tweeting resumed.

January 7: "I've had to put up with the Fake News from the first day I announced that I would be running for President. Now I have to put up with a Fake Book, written by a totally discredited author. Ronald Reagan had the same problem and handled it well. So will I!"

Last, on January 13: "So much Fake News is being reported. They don't even try to get it right, or correct it when they are wrong. They promote the Fake Book of a mentally deranged author, who knowingly writes false information. The Mainstream Media is crazed that WE won the election!"

I recall that last one specifically because I was about to go on Fox News to discuss Hawaii's state government mistakenly alerting residence of an incoming ballistic missile, which had just happened that day. So, I checked Trump's feed to see if he had said anything about it right before I went on air. Nope, just more about Wolff's book. It was apparently so important, he shared that tweet again the following day with a re-tweet of himself.

Many of Trump's observations in his tweets about the book were explicitly true. Reagan really did endure make-believe speculation from the media about his mental capacity that was intended to politically damage him. Wolff really is a widely untrusted writer. Bannon really does look like a slob.

But if there ever was a need to make the case that President Trump was mentally incapacitated, these tweets would undoubtedly be presented in court for their sheer obsessive quantity.

Both during his campaign and during his presidency, Trump has shown an acute sense for what animates normal, working people, something the media are never able to do. This was one of the few times he was wandering aimlessly in the media's bubble, fighting a fight almost exclusively of interest to journalists. The only person with everything to gain from the conflict: Wolff.

CHAPTER 9
DR. RONNY JACKSON'S ANTIDOTE

It didn't need to be done, but the White House sent out Trump's personal physician, Dr. Ronny Jackson, a Navy rear admiral, to fully shut down Wolff's absurd and oft-repeated assertions that the president is mentally incapacitated.

On January 16, Jackson spent more than one hour answering every serious question ("Can you assess the president's mental fitness for office?") and every stupid curiosity ("Is he limited to one scoop of ice cream now?") that White House reporters could come up with pertaining to the president's health.

The result was a complete refutation of the most sensational element of Wolff's book.

Jackson read the results of Trump's physical, which revealed that the 71-year-old male is a little flabby, should eat less processed food, and needs to add cardio to his routine.

In other words, Trump is an average elderly American.

According to the doctor's statement, Trump takes medicine daily to lower his cholesterol, aspirin to maintain heart health, and a multivitamin. He also uses a cream to treat a common skin condition and takes a pill that delays male pattern baldness.

"The president's overall health is excellent," Dr. Jackson said.

And on whether Trump is mentally diminished, he said the president requested a test that could demonstrate he isn't. Jackson said based on his year-long acquaintance and working relationship with Trump, he saw no reason to conduct a test but did it anyway.

The president took the Montreal Cognitive Assessment, which asks subjects a series of basic questions that test math, memory, and motor skills. He got a perfect score, and Dr. Jackson said he saw no reason to administer any further testing.

"So, the fact that the president got 30 out of 30 on that exam, I think that there's no indication whatsoever that he has any cognitive issues," said Dr. Jackson, who had also served as former President Obama's physician. "And, on a day-to-day basis, like I said before, it's been my experience that the president—he's very sharp, and he's very articulate when he speaks to me....I've found no reason to think that the President has any issues whatsoever with his thought process."

This is in direct contrast to *Fire and Fury*'s claim that Trump is in the office staring at the wall with his mouth open. But, because so many in the national media had hung their hopes and dreams on the book, they reacted by shooting ink from their sacs.

The New York Times commissioned an op-ed from Steven Buser, who co-edited a book that compiled a bunch of anti-Trump essays casting the president as a "clear and present danger." Buser's *Times* piece acknowledged the normal cognitive results but pointed out one very big flaw: *Trump's doctor said he may be okay but would be pass an exam to physically handle nuclear weapons?!*

"I have not had the opportunity to examine the president personally, but warning signs abound," wrote Buser. "What if I had reliable outside information that [a hypothetical] Airman Trump displayed erratic emotions? That I saw very clearly that he was engaging in cyberbullying on Twitter? That he had repeatedly made untruthful or highly distorted statements?...These are the sorts of things that set off alarms for Air Force psychiatrists."[89]

Setting aside that Trump has never "cyberbullied" anyone, Buser's comparison would be somewhat compelling if the president had ever shown an excitement for getting his hands on a nuke. He may be the one person who can now give the order to launch one but, by retired Marine Gen. John Kelly's account, Trump has every aversion to them.

During a press briefing in October 2017, Kelly, now serving as White House chief of staff with an impeccable four-decade military career behind him, responded to a report that said Trump had wanted to increase the U.S. nuclear arsenal by tenfold.

"You know, I would tell you this," said Kelly, "in spite of what someone reported the other day about the president—and I don't think he'd mind my sharing this, what he said to me many, many times and to the group oftentimes—I hear him most say, about nuclear weapons, that wouldn't it be great if we could get rid of them all, as opposed to we need 10 times more."[90]

Speaking on CNN the day after Dr. Jackson's briefing, the network's chief medical correspondent Sanjay Gupta said the physical test results actually showed Trump is afflicted with a heart malady. "A few years ago, dating back to 2009, President Trump started having these tests that are actually looking for the presence of calcium in the blood vessels that lead to the heart…and steadily, up until just this past week, when he had them performed again, those numbers have gone up," said Gupta. "Well, when they get to a certain range, and his number is in the 130s, that means he has heart disease."[91]

Gupta is specialized in neurology, not cardiology, and he has never treated the president, though it's worth noting he was under consideration in 2009 as then-President Obama's pick for U.S. Surgeon General and he deserves a Lifetime Achievement award for his gravity-defying ability to explain away the millions of people losing their existing health insurance plans under Obamacare.

"So those plans are essentially not available anymore," Gupta said in 2013. "They're technically illegal plans. And if people had those plans, those are the plans that are no longer available and they're being told they have got to get a new plan.… I don't think this has been explained very well to people."[92]

Oh, so it's okay that Obama lied when he said Obamacare wouldn't disrupt anyone's existing insurance plans or their choice of doctor? *Makes sense! Thanks, Sanjay!*

With that kind of analysis, it's no wonder he's on CNN rather than, say, saving lives.

On MSNBC, Trump's normal bill of health inspired *Morning Joe* co-host Mika Brzezinski to take a break from tilting her head and quizzically squinting her eyes at the camera so that she could discount all of it.

Speaking at a depressed crawl and with her voice an octave lower than normal, Brzezinski went through the details of the healthy report on the January 17 edition of *Morning Joe*, before stating, "I'm not really sure if it makes me feel better that this doctor says that he has no cognitive issues. It makes me feel worse and more worried for the country."

As if to question whether Jackson really is in fact a doctor, Brzezinski's co-host and fiancé Joe Scarborough jumped in to cast further doubt about Trump's normal cognitive status. "If that is the case," Scarborough said, "and medically, perhaps, that is, [Jackson] has shocked and surprised a lot of people who have worked around [Trump] for the past several years, who have been saying that he is not."

Two days later, the sting in hearing from a renowned doctor that the president was relatively healthy and not crazy had completely settled in. Scarborough went hysterical on his show, noting that Dr.

Jackson found nothing wrong with Trump's admitted four to five hours of nightly sleep.

It must be a hoax!

"You won't find a reputable doctor in America that will tell you getting four hours of sleep a night is good for you!" screamed Scarborough. "They will all say the same thing: Get four hours of sleep a night, your cognitive ability starts to degenerate. Not a single respectable doctor in America would say what he said. So are we questioning his integrity? No, we're not. I'm just questioning his motivations. Because maybe he likes eating at the White House [inaudible]. I don't know why. But his own words are not the words of a physician. They're the words of a political hack....Come on, that's just shameful."

Because Dr. Jackson hadn't come out to announce Trump's official commitment to Bellevue, he was a "political hack." This is what we call a public meltdown. The derangement is so strong in some corners of the national media that they're even willing to reject the sound assessment of a respected doctor.

Wolff's campaign to promote his book by convincing the country that their president was brain dead was shocking and relentless. On NBC's *Meet the Press*, he had said that the 25th Amendment, wherein the president's cabinet can vote to remove him from office, "is [a] concept that is alive every day in the White House."[93]

He said on PBS that "anything [Trump] does worries [the White House staff] because it is always unpredictable. It's always unpredictable, it's extreme, it's exceptional and it is outside the bounds of what one has traditionally done as the president of the United States." Wolff said that "the people closest to the president" are "afraid…for the country."[94]

He said on NBC's *Today* that "100 percent of the people around him" question Trump's stability.[95]

He told CNN's Don Lemon that he found it "alarming that, as everyone on his staff does, that he repeats and repeats and repeats the same thing in the same conversation," a phenomenon that, Wolff said, amounted to a "crisis."[96]

But Trump's repetition, and the other qualities that distinguish his speech, has been rationally explained by John McWhorter, an actual linguist and professor at Columbia University. McWhorter wrote in a contributed piece for the *Times* in February that Trump's speech patterns are the result of someone who speaks casually, informally, and with confidence that people understand his intent.

To put it another way: Trump speaks like a human and not like whatever Hillary Clinton is.

Comparing public remarks by Trump from decades ago to more recent ones, McWhorter humorously wrote, "The difference between the younger man talking in sentences and the older one talking in vocal ejaculations is evidence not of decline but authenticity—he has settled into his normal. Late in life an artless man has learned that he could leave his linguistic fly unzipped and life would go on. It may not be pretty, but it isn't a sign that his pants are going to fall down."[97]

Whatever Wolff had written in his book of the president's psychological health, it had been undone by Dr. Jackson's medical exam made available for the public to see for itself.

Not everyone in the media was ready to let it go because they so needed Wolff's claims to be true. But more honest voices in the press rejected Wolff's assertions that titillated commentators and talk show hosts who write embarrassing country songs on the side.

Trump is "the same person who I was interviewing six years ago," *New York Times* reporter Maggie Haberman, who previously covered Trump for the *New York Post* tabloid, said in a podcast interview in January 2017.[98]

Matt Drudge, editor and founder of the influential *Drudge Report*, may be a Trump supporter in general, but his website still gave substantial publicity to Wolff's book by linking to dozens of stories about it. Even so, after Wolff said in one interview that Trump doesn't even want to be president, Drudge tweeted that it's finally "time to call out Michael Wolff and his fabricated bullshit!"[99]

The tweet continued, "I had dinner with the president a few weeks ago and he was in fine form. He was optimistic, engaged, on top of the world, loving the job. And already talking about his 2020 re-election run!!"

Haberman and Drudge are two people who actually know Trump. The president frequently rings up Haberman unsolicited and on the record to talk about whatever is on his mind. Drudge has been in touch with Trump and his team since the campaign. Funny that the people who actually know Trump know that he's not retarded.

CHAPTER 10

FRAUD AND FICTION REDUX

After being willfully played by Michael Wolff, it's clear the national media largely have no intent to make any serious adjustments that might show they're ready to understand what Trump's election says about the state of America right now. You can see it in ongoing coverage of the Russia investigations that polls show Americans somewhat care about yet care less about than other issues when compared.

A Politico-Morning Consult poll conducted in late October said that just 35 percent of registered voters nationally believe the Russia investigation should be "a top priority" for Congress.[100] That's in contrast to 37 percent who said passing an immigration reform bill should be a top priority; 39 percent who said reforming entitlements like Social Security and Medicare should be a top priority; and 42 percent who said passing a tax reform bill should be a top priority.

But how the national media reacted to indictments against thirteen Russians in February 2018 is a case study in how the media react to almost everything in Trump politics. It's full hysteria, followed by people who actually know things explaining that what just happened isn't what the press told you. And when the press come to accept reality, they shift the subject.

After news broke of the indictments, HBO's *Real Time* host Bill Maher said, "I just want to ask the Trump voters, what is left for you? He's plainly a traitor who doesn't defend his own country. This is not a hoax. This really happened…and [the Russians] were trying to get Trump elected."[101]

New York Times columnist Thomas Friedman said the indictments showed that "President Trump is either totally compromised by the Russians or is a towering fool, or both." He also suggested Trump must be "hiding something" and that because he hasn't reacted with full hostility to Russia's election meddling his "behavior amounts to a refusal to carry out his oath of office—to protect and defend the Constitution."[102]

Protect and defend from what?

The indictments related to more than a dozen Russians and three companies that stand accused of attempting to disrupt the election. The charges said that the Russians deliberately agitated voters by using social media to spread content on controversial issues, like the Black Lives Matter movement. Prosecutors also said the accused stole the identities of American citizens and posed as political activists in carrying out the plot. The charges very explicitly did not implicate the Trump campaign, even though it said that some of the Russians, while posing as Americans, helped organize pro-Trump rallies.

Yet the indictments also noted that the Russians organized at least one anti-Trump rally as well. The conspiracy, according to the charges, began four years ago in 2014. Trump launched his campaign for the Republican nomination in the summer of 2015. This "conspiracy" could be carried out by anyone with too much time in their trailer home. In fact, it sounds a lot like what Americans with too much time *have* been doing in their trailer homes.

Russians set up Facebook pages and Twitter accounts to spread dumb memes telling blacks not to vote, promoting Trump and calling Hillary Clinton "Satan."

Okay. And *Bloomberg Businessweek*'s Joshua Green, an American, wrote a whole book about Trump and former White House strategist Steve Bannon called *Devil's Bargain*. Demonic references in politics are trite, and where's the evidence they ever changed anyone's vote?

If an entire government like Russia's wants to tip America's democracy, posting notes on Facebook isn't the most novel approach. The indictments said the Russians wanted to divide Americans. Americans are already divided, so they should have saved their money.

Scheming to create division in America is like creating a plot to turn it up a few degrees in hell. What's the point? It's hell, dummy.

You would hope other countries stay out of our elections, but if this is the extent of it, how is Trump expected to react? He didn't tweet about Vladimir Putin, so Friedman likened it to former President George W. Bush if he had ignored September 11.

With stunning originality, *Washington Post* writer Max Boot made the same comparison. "That's roughly where we stand after the second-worst foreign attack on America in the past two decades," Boot wrote. "The Russian subversion of the 2016 election did not, to be sure, kill nearly 3,000 people. But its longer-term impact may be even more corrosive by undermining faith in our democracy....The most benign explanation is that [Trump] is putting his vanity—he can't have anything taint his glorious victory—above his obligation to 'protect and defend the Constitution.' The more sinister hypothesis is that he has something to hide and, having benefited from Russia's assistance once, hopes for more aid in 2018 and 2020."[103]

After a few days, the delirium tapered, and journalists found a new reason to be angry at Trump and the indictments that had nothing to do with his campaign colluding with Russia. "One thing that is clear to me following the special counsel's indictment of thirteen Russians and three companies for interfering with our election is that the black vote was specifically under attack, from sources foreign and domestic," wrote Charles Blow, formerly a graphics designer for *The New York Times* now entrusted for unknown reasons to write political commentary. He was referring to the Russian Facebook posts and tweets that told blacks to simply not vote, something even rapper Killer Mike and former NFL player Colin Kaepernick told blacks to do! And which Blow even acknowledged in the column![104]

The Washington Post's Dana Milbank said the Russian conspiracy turned Americans who supported Trump into "useful idiots."[105]

Because the election didn't go the way they wanted, it must have been a trick!

There was no trick. And if there were, the indictments against the Russians expressly showed that it wasn't Trump's. That's true even if the media won't accept it.

It confounded reporters and TV commentators without critical thinking skills (take your pick of the list of CNN contributors) that people just didn't care about Stormy Daniels, the porn actress President Trump allegedly paid off to keep quiet before the 2016 election.

The media want to know: *Why didn't this story hurt him?!*

The answer is simple: 1) everyone knows Trump has a tacky history; voters chose him anyway, and 2) by the way, we have a country we're trying to save here!

Point one still scandalizes the media, but the rest of the country has its eyes on point two.

The Wall Street Journal broke the news on January 12 that Trump's lawyer, Michael Cohen, in October 2016 allegedly arranged for a 130,000-dollar payment to Stephanie Clifford, Daniels's real name, in exchange for her silence about an affair the two had more than a decade ago.[106] Unfortunately for the White House, which continues to deny Trump and Daniels had an affair, almost every legal settlement related to sex is null and void because their details are now routinely leaked to the press.

Emboldened by the *Journal*'s report, *In Touch Weekly* published a 2011 interview with Daniels wherein she described sexual encounters with Trump.[107]

CNN's Chris Cillizza gave it the old college try at political analysis again, writing that "it's hard to argue that an unexplained six-figure payment from his personal lawyer to a porn star in the runup [sic] to the election doesn't warrant more attention—and more answers—than we are currently getting."[108]

The Washington Post, where anti-Trump conservatives are always welcome, published an op-ed by Erick Erickson where he said, "The conservatives who 20 years ago wanted to chase President Bill Clinton out of town for having sex in the Oval Office are now trying to ignore the current president reportedly cheating on his current wife with a porn star."[109]

The New York Times's affirmative action hire Charles Blow wrote, "If this were Barack Obama, Tiki-torch-toting Nazis would have descended on the White House and burned it to the ground. Not only that, America's racist folks masquerading as religious folks would have used Obama's moral failing as proof of a black pathology."[110]

Setting aside the media narrative that every day under Trump is Selma, the difference between the current president and the last one is that Trump was no one's idea of a Christian family man. *The New York Post* never ran a photo of former President Barack Obama on its cover next to the headline: "Best Sex I've Ever Had." That was Trump, and people knew this is what they were getting when they set out to vote on Election Day in 2016.

The difference between the current president and Bill Clinton is that Clinton was in the White House taking advantage of an intern. The alleged affair with Trump and Daniels is more than a decade old and—*she's a porn actress!*

Context matters. Like in 2015 during the first Republican primary debate, when Megyn Kelly confronted Trump with a series of comments he had made about some women, including, "Must be a pretty picture, you dropping to your knees."

Kelly didn't mention it, but the comment was made during an episode of *Celebrity Apprentice* to Brande Roderick—a *Playboy* model who was literally paid to pose on her knees for a pretty picture.[111] Moreover, Trump's campaign message—that the country was in desperate need of a course change—was endorsed by voters who share the urgency.

That his supporters, including evangelicals, were willing to overlook Trump's gaudy past in favor of his policies on immigration, the economy, and Islamic terrorism, demonstrates how powerful those issues are and how well Trump captures the national mood.

The media don't understand why the Stormy Daniels story didn't engulf the White House. They don't understand why wall-to-wall coverage of the Russia investigation isn't interesting to most people. That's because they didn't understand the issues Trump won with America.

They still don't.

In place of that crucial understanding are only fraud and fiction.

ACKNOWLEDGMENTS

There are countless thanks I could give out for the tips, help, and feedback I received from friends, family, and colleagues for this book. To name a few, thanks to my publisher, David Bernstein, who was an absolute pleasure to work with. To Mom and Dad for their endless support in everything. To Theodore and Bear: Getting to do this at the side of you both made it a breeze. To Ann Coulter and Jeffrey Lord, two of America's lasting and brilliant political writers, for their contributions to the book. And many thanks to the very few journalists who knew that *Fire and Fury* was purely fraud and fiction from the beginning; the footnotes relied on much of your work, and I'm grateful for your insights.

ABOUT THE AUTHOR

Eddie Scarry is a journalist in Washington, D.C., where he writes on media and politics for the *Washington Examiner*. He is a frequent guest on Fox News and his work has also appeared in the *New York Post*, *Real Clear Politics*, and *Mediaite.com*.

ENDNOTES

1 "*Fire and Fury* is No. 1 on *USA TODAY*'s list as Trump book sets sales records," *USA Today*, Jan. 11, 2018.

2 "The Wolff eats its own," *The New York Times*' Bret Stephens, Jan. 11, 2018.

3 "Let's Elect Hillary Now," *The Wall Street Journal*'s Bret Stephens, Dec. 21, 2015.

4 "My Former Republican Party," *The Wall Street Journal*'s Bret Stephens, Oct. 25, 2016.

5 "Everyone in Trumpworld knows he's an idiot," *The New York Times*' Michelle Goldberg, Jan. 4, 2018.

6 "Franken should go," *The New York Times*' Michelle Goldberg, Nov. 16, 2017.

7 "When our allies are accused of harassment," *The New York Times*' Michelle Goldberg, Nov. 20, 2017.

8 "MSNBC guest wonders if Trump has erectile dysfunction," *Washington Examiner*, Sep. 15, 2016.

9 "*Morning Joe* contemplates Trump's mental 'stability' after dry-mouth speech," *Washington Examiner*, Dec. 7, 2017.

10 "White House doctor: Trump slurred speech because of dry mouth," *Washington Examiner*, Jan. 16, 2018.

11 "I asked Trump a blunt question: Do you read?" *The Washington Post's* Joe Scarborough, Jan. 4, 2018.

12 ibid.

13 "From *Fire and Fury* to political firestorm," *The New York Times'* Jonathan Martin, Jan. 8, 2018.

14 "Affidavit of Samuel D. Nunberg in support of stay of arbitration proceedings," Supreme Court of the State of New York, County of New York, June 2016.

15 "Al Sharpton Accepts Apology from Donald Trump Aide Who Was Fired Over Racial Posts," *The New York Times*, Aug. 3, 2015.

16 "Trump campaign staffers get into public screaming match," *New York Post*, May 19, 2016.

17 "Here's What We Know About the Membership of Mar-a-Lago," *Town and Country*, Oct. 9, 2017.

18 "*CNN's* Jim Acosta claims victory in briefing beef with Stephen Miller: 'He couldn't take that kind of heat,'" *Washington Examiner*, Aug. 2, 2017.

19 "The Foreign-Born Population in the United States," United States Census Bureau, Dec. 2, 2011.

20 "U.S. Satisfaction with Immigration Levels Reaches New High," Gallup, Jan. 18, 2017.

21 "Good example of something that's patently false/absurd," Twitter, @elianayjohnson, Jan. 5, 2018.

22   "Don't go to *Morning Joe* for mental health evaluations about Trump (or anyone else)," *Washington Examiner's* Eddie Scarry, June 10, 2017.

23   "*Morning Joe* co-host: Trump may be 'mentally ill,'" The Hill, June 8, 2017.

24   "Again, Trump is *not well* and he is getting worse by the day, according to those on the inside," Twitter, @joenbc, May 15, 2017.

25   "He is not well," Twitter, @joenbc, May 11, 2017.

26   "Trump is getting even Trumpier!," *The New York Times'* David Brooks, July 19, 2016.

27   John Boehner talks election, time in office," *The Stanford Daily*, April 28, 2016.

28   "Donald Trump eyes 2016," *National Review*, June 3, 2013.

29   "Donald Trump didn't want to be president," Michael Wolff in New York, Jan. 3, 2018.

30   "Press conference minutes in 2016: Trump 278, Clinton 38," *Washington Examiner*, Sep. 9, 2016.

31   "Donald Trump: Bill Clinton 'Fair Game' For Criticism on Campaign Trail," *TODAY*, YouTube, Dec. 29, 2015.

32   "Exclusive: Trump is ready to 'get in gear,'" *Washington Examiner*, July 18, 2016.

33   "*Morning Joe* Michael Wolff Cold Open – SNL," YouTube, Jan. 13, 2018.

34 "POTUS Print Pool 12 & 13," On-duty White House pool reporter Todd J. Gillman, Jan. 20, 2017.

35 "Pool report 15/motorcade ready and MLK bust correction," On-duty White House pool reporter Todd J. Gillman, Jan. 20, 2017.

36 "A note to our readers," *Time's* Nancy Gibbs, Jan. 24, 2017.

37 "Trump feeds fish, winds up pouring entire box of food into koi pond," *CNN*, Nov. 6, 2017.

38 "Donald Trump and the fish food dump: How early reports got it wrong," PolitiFact, Nov. 6, 2017.

39 "Northern New Jersey draws probers' eyes," *The Washington Post's* Serge Kovaleski, Sep. 18, 2001.

40 "What Trump is really saying in his tweets: I'm weak," *The Washington Post's* Eugene Robinson, Jan. 9, 2017.

41 "Meryl Streep Calls Out Donald Trump for Mocking Disabled Reporter in Riveting Golden Globes Speech," The Daily Beast, Jan. 8, 2017.

42 "Streep vs. Trump for America," *The New York Times'* Roger Cohen, Jan. 10, 2017.

43 "Where is Serge Kovaleski - The 'Investigative' Reporter' That's Hiding in the Shadows," YouTube, Jan. 9, 2017.

44 "Did Trump really mock reporter's disability?" YouTube, Sep. 14, 2016.

45 "Reality Check: What do countries spend on climate fund?" *BBC*, June 2, 2017.

46 "Zakaria: 'United States Resigned as Leader of The Free World' When Trump Left Paris Climate Agreement," RealClearPolitics, June 2, 2017.

47 "Trump turns his back on the world," *The Washington Post*, June 1, 2017.

48 MSNBC, June 1, 2017.

49 "Reluctant signatory India takes moral high-ground on Paris climate deal," *CNN*, June 2, 2017.

50 "Western values increasingly endangered by terrorism and extremism, Trump warns Europe," *The Washington Post*, July 6, 2017.

51 "Trump's dangerous thirst for a clash of civilizations," *The Washington Post's* Eugene Robinson, July 6, 2017.

52 "Trump's white-nationalist dog whistles in Warsaw," *The Washington Post's* Jonathan Capehart, July 6, 2017.

53 "Trump's speech in Poland sounded like an alt-right manifesto," Vox's Sarah Wildman, July 6, 2017.

54 "North Korea warns 'hundreds of millions' in US will DIE if 'Trump doesn't prevent war,'" *The Daily Express*, May 12, 2017. Accessed at https://www.express.co.uk/news/world/803077/

55 "The First Lady of Poland Smoothly Avoided Shaking Donald Trump's Hand," *Vanity Fair*, July 6, 2017.

56 "OHMYGODOHMYGODOHMYGODOHMYGODOHMYGOD," Twitter, @CillizzaCNN, July 6, 2017.

57 "Meet the world's leaders in hypocrisy," *The New York Times'* Nicholas Kristof, Sep. 21, 2017.

58 "Are we down to President Pence?" *The New York Times'* Gail Collins, Sep. 21, 2017.

59 "At the United Nations, Trump tries to out-bluff 'rocket man,'" *USA Today*, Sep. 19, 2017. Accessed at https://www.usatoday.com/story/opinion/2017/09/19/united-nations-trump-tries-out-bluff-rocket-man-editorials-debates/681461001/

60 "ABC's Terry Moran: Trump's North Korea Talk Borders on 'Threat of Committing a War Crime,'" Mediaite, Sept. 19, 2017.

61 "At UN Trump threatened to commit a war crime: 'totally destroy North Korea,'" Twitter, @Lawrence, Sep. 19, 2017.

62 "Gee, Kim Jon-un is so irrational for wanting nuclear weapons," Twitter, @jessicaschul, Sep. 19, 2017.

63 "Uhhhh. Kim Jung's letter to @realDonaldTrump is a little bit more sane than @realDonaldTrump. Maybe we trade?" Twitter, @chelseahandler, Sep. 21, 2017.

64 "Trump Tower meeting with Russians 'treasonous', Bannon says in explosive book," *The Guardian*, Jan. 3, 2018.

65 "Steve Bannon, unrepentant," *American Prospect*, Aug. 16, 2017.

66 "You Can't Make This S— Up: My Year Inside Trump's Insane White House," *Hollywood Reporter's* Michael Wolff, Jan. 4, 2018.

67 "Reince Priebus is ousted amid stormy days for White House," *The New York Times*, July 28, 2017.

68 "Edward Klein defends his Obama biography, *The Amateur*," *The Washington Post*, June 19, 2012.

69 "If You Were So Inclined, You Could Stick It on a Bumper," *The New York Times*, May 16, 2012.

70 "Why believe Michael Wolff? Because, for now, this stuff is too good not to," *Los Angeles Times'* Virginia Heffernan, Jan. 4, 2018.

71 "How ex-spy Christopher Steele compiled his explosive Trump-Russia dossier," *Vanity Fair's* Howard Blum, April 2017 edition. Accessed at https://www.vanity-fair.com/news/2017/03/how-the-explosive-russian-dossier-was-compiled-christopher-steele

72 "'Complete invention:' Blair denies telling Trump UK may have spied on him," *The Guardian*, Jan. 4, 2018. Accessed at https://www.theguardian.com/us-news/2018/jan/04/tony-blair-donald-trump-gchq-spied

73 "*Fire & Fury* Author Michael Wolff Claims Trump Is Having an Affair: 'Read Between the Lines,'" *People*, Jan. 22, 2018.

74 "Michael Wolff is 'absolutely sure' Trump is currently having an affair," *Vanity Fair*, Jan. 20, 2018.

75 "Michael Wolff claims Trump is having an affair: 'Read between the lines,'" *Entertainment Weekly*, Jan. 20, 2018.

76 "An affair with Trump? Nikki Haley on 'disgusting' rumors and her rise to a top foreign policy role," *Politico*, Jan. 26, 2018.

77 "Michael Wolff, *Fire and Fury*, theSkimm, Sip 'n Skimm," YouTube, Jan. 30, 2018.

78 "No, Michael Wolff, it was not fun for Nikki Haley to have to deny the sexist and unfounded rumors you floated that she was having an affair with her boss, the President of the United States," Twitter, @elise_jordan, Jan. 31, 2018.

79 "This is so vile," Twitter, @jaketapper, Jan. 31, 2018.

80 Reporter tells *Fire and Fury* author Michael Wolff to remove him from book's acknowledgments," *Washington Examiner*, Jan. 31, 2018.

81 "Wolff trapped," New Republic, Aug. 30, 2004.

82 "Michael Wolff is crumbling before our eyes," *The Washington Post's* Erik Wemple, Feb. 26, 2018.

83 "An update for this thread: Wolff acknowledges mixing up Mark Berman (me) and Mike Berman (not me), apologizes for that error in the book," Twitter, @markberman, Jan. 7, 2018.

84 "Wolff is a talented writer and has undeniable observational gifts; but this 'too good to check' reporting is a disgrace. Most of us work hard to make sure we can verify facts before printing them. Yes we screw up sometimes but it's devastating for us when we do," Twitter, @jonathanvswan, Jan. 6, 2018.

85 "Gay conservatives who helped kickstart Trump's GOP career have serious regrets," *CNN*, March 3, 2016.

86 "Michael Wolff's book on Trump sells a million copies," *The Wall Street Journal*, Jan. 10, 2018.

87 "President Trump tries to quash bombshell book," *CNN*, Jan. 4, 2018.

88   *"Fire and Fury* Publisher Moves Publication Date to Tomorrow," *Deadline Hollywood*, Jan. 4, 2018.

89   "Would the Air Force let Airman Trump near a nuclear weapon?" Steven Buser contributing to *The New York Times*, Jan. 17, 2018.

90   White House press briefing, press secretary Sarah Sanders and White House Chief-of-Staff Gen. John Kelly, Oct. 12, 2017.

91   "*CNN's* Sanjay Gupta disputes Trump's personal doctor: 'He does have heart disease,'" *Washington Examiner*, Jan. 17, 2018.

92   "*CNN's* Gupta on ObamaCare Dropping Millions from Health Plans: 'It Hasn't Been Explained Very Well,'" NewsBusters, Oct. 30, 2013.

93   "*Fire and Fury* author Wolff says 25th Amendment concept 'alive every day' at White House," *NBC News*, Jan. 7, 2018.

94   "Trump insiders 'afraid for the country,' says Michael Wolff," *PBS*, Jan. 8, 2018.

95   "Michael Wolff says he 'absolutely' spoke to President Trump for his tell-all book," *NBC News*, Jan. 5, 2018.

96   "Lemon to Michael Wolff: Is Trump book gossip or journalism?" YouTube, Jan. 9, 2018.

97   "What Trump's speech says about his mental fitness," John McWhorter contributing to *The New York Times*, Feb. 6, 2018.

98   "Wonder Woman: Maggie Haberman," Maggie Haberman on *The Katie Couric Podcast*, Jan. 18, 2018.

99   "Matt Drudge slams Michael Wolff's 'fabricated bulls—t,' says Trump is 'in fine form,'" *Washington Examiner*, Jan. 23, 2018.

100 "Morning Consult – Politico National Tracking Poll," Oct. 17, 2016.

101 "HBO's *Real Time with Bill Maher*," Feb. 16, 2018.

102 "Whatever Trump Is Hiding Is Hurting All of Us Now," *The New York Times'* Thomas Friedman, Feb. 18, 2018.

103 "Trump is ignoring the worst attack on America since 9/11," *The Washington Post's* Max Boot, Feb. 18, 2018.

104 "Attacking the 'woke' black vote," *The New York Times'* Charles Blow, Feb. 18, 2018.

105 "Putin's useful idiots," *The Washington Post's* Dana Milbank, Feb. 20, 2018.

106 "Trump Lawyer Arranged $130,000 Payment for Adult-Film Star's Silence," *The Wall Street Journal*, Jan. 12, 2018.

107 "Stormy Daniels' Explosive Full Interview on Donald Trump Affair: 'I Can Describe His Junk Perfectly' (*Exclusive*)," *In Touch*, Feb. 14, 2018.

108 "The Stormy Daniels story should be a bigger deal," *CNN's* Chris Cillizza, Jan. 19, 2018.

109 "Trump's short-term achievements will cost conservatives," Erick Erickson in *The Washington Post*, Jan. 19, 2018.

110 "Soul of a Nation," *The New York Times'* Charles Blow, Jan. 25, 2018.

111 "Trump Told Female 'Apprentice' to 'Drop to Your Knees,'" The Daily Beast, Aug. 7, 2015.

Made in the USA
Lexington, KY
04 April 2018